Sleep as a State of Consciousness in Advaita Vedānta

Sleep as a State of Consciousness in Advaita Vedānta

Arvind Sharma

State University of New York Press

Published by
State University of New York Press, Albany

Printed in the United States of America

For information, address the State University of New York Press,
90 State Street, Suite 700, Albany, NY 12207

Production by Diane Ganeles
Marketing by Anne M. Valentine

Library of Congress Cataloging-in-Publication Data

Sharma, Arvind.
Sleep as a state of consciousness in Advaita Vedānta / Arvind Sharma.
p. cm.
Includes bibliographical references and index.
ISBN 0-7914-6251-X (hardcover: alk. paper)
1. Advaita. 2. Philosophy, Hindu. 3. Sleep—Religious aspects—Hinduism. I. Title.
B132.A3S43 2004
154.6'0954—dc22 2003069326

10 9 8 7 6 5 4 3 2 1

Contents

Preface

Advaita Vedānta is a well-known philosophical system of India. One of the well-known doctrines associated with Advaita Vedānta is that of *avasthātraya*, or of the three states of consciousness: waking (*jāgrat*), dreaming (*svapna*), and deep sleep (*suṣupti*). Out of these three states of daily experience, Advaita Vedānta often draws on that of deep sleep to validate an argument, point a moral, or even adorn a tale.

Despite this heavy reliance on the phenomenon of deep sleep in Advaita Vedānta, no broad-based study of it seems to have been undertaken from an Advaitic point of view. (If such an investigation has indeed been undertaken, I am not aware of it). This monograph is an attempt at such an analysis. As it tries to bring together several viewpoints under one cover, it is also an attempt at synthesis.

There are, I believe, good reasons for undertaking this exercise. It might be of interest to those who work within Advaita Vedānta. It might also be of interest to those who work more broadly in the field of Vedānta. The doctrine of *avasthātraya* and the associated *catuṣpāda* doctrine, although important for Advaitic thought, are not confined to it. They are shared by other schools of Vedānta. The monograph may also be of interest to those who work even more generally in the field of Hindu philosophy, for some of the differences among these schools turn on their analysis of deep sleep. The system of Yoga, for instance, speaks of *nidrā* or sleep as one of the five *cittavṛttis* or cognitive mental states.[1] Moreover, the argument it employs for postulating some form of continuous consciousness is also similar to the one employed in Advaita.[2] However, while in Advaita the argument ultimately points to the reality of *ātman* (or more precisely the *ātman* as *sākṣī*), which is ultimately "without a second," in Yoga it points to the reality of the *puruṣa,* of whom there are many.[3]

The relevance of a work such as this on Advaita Vedānta may even extend beyond the confines of Hindu philosophy, to those of Indian philosophy. The apparent cessation of consciousness in sleep serves to illustrate Buddhist ideas of a discontinuous but connected flow of consciousness, while it points in an opposite direction in Advaita. It is illuminating that some Buddhists even consider this difference a minor error (*alpāparādha*) on the part of Advaitins, apparently something not worth losing sleep over.

Beyond Indian philosophy, this exercise may interest those who work in philosophy in general, as well as those who don't work within it but attend to it. For it lifts up for consideration the relationship between philosophy and physiology. One might propose, for instance, at the risk of sounding reductionistic, that all, or most, of philosophical speculation has a physiological basis, that philosophizing about death is based on *fear* of death; that *thirst* for knowledge is merely the philosophical expression of a psychological drive, or that the concept of objectless consciousness is only the philosophized version of sleep. Alternatively, one might turn the tables and maintain, like the Advaitin, that the phenomenon of sleep is only a physiological earnest of a metaphysical reality. After all, empirically one cannot hope for absolute intimations, only intimations of the Absolute.

The exercise may also not be without relevance for the comparative study of religion. An investigation of the nature of sleep, and deep or dreamless sleep in Advaita Vedānta may

> also illumine prevalent Western assumptions about consciousness states and "reality". To our "common sense", it seems absurd to argue that sleep reveals the true nature of things while waking is at bottom delusive. To

> advaitins, however, the blurring of inner ("psychic") appearance and outer ("physical") appearance in dream (and the total collapse of such distinctions in sleep) reveals a fundamental truth (non-duality), not a lessened grasp on reality.
>
> From a different "common sense", dreams suggest a "reality" (taken to be the external physical world) which is merely a mental creation. As dreamers believe their dreams are real (and not merely their mental creations), we now believe waking is real, and not such a creation. From waking state, we "know" dreams aren't real; in the same way, once we become *brahman*, we will know waking is not real. Thus, one should not aim for waking's critical self-awareness, but for "awakening" from the "dream" (or nightmare!) of daylight vicissitudes.[4]

Finally, the exercise may even be significant in the study of psychology, as offering another perspective on 'altered states of consciousness.'[5] After all, sleep is a 'state of altered consciousness' that occupies a third of one's life!

Enough said. This is the spirit in which the monograph is being offered, and I hope will be welcomed as such.

Introduction

I

This monograph deals with the question of sleep in Advaita Vedānta. But the theme presupposes that the phenomenon of sleep is an issue of some kind for Advaita Vedānta in particular, or Indian philosophy in general. For the reader who does not share this presupposition, such questions as the following will naturally arise: 'Why should philosophers be concerned with sleep as an epistemological or religious problem? Why are the Indian philosophers concerned with it? Why do Advaita philosophers view sleep as an important philosophical dilemma, and why are they losing sleep over it?'

II

The question as to why philosophers in general should be concerned with the phenomenon of sleep can be answered in two ways, one reductive and the other nonreductive.

According to the reductive view the superstructures of thought raised by philosophers have physiological bases, and one cannot avoid this issue by retreating into intellectual loftiness and claiming that our powers of intellection are immune to such influences. If this reductive line of reasoning is pursued further, it will lead to the suggestion that the philosophical idea of a nondual reality may be rooted in the physiological phenomenon of deep sleep, wherein such a nonduality is actually experienced by human beings. The other, nonreductive approach will also hark to the same point but this time use the phenomenon of sleep not to *account for* the claim of a nonduality reality, but as an everyday *illustration* that might reinforce its philosophical credibility.

III

Any attempt to answer the other questions raised earlier in section I above, must involve a brief account of the doctrine of three states of consciousness, or *avasthātraya*, as it is formally known, within the school of Hindu philosophy called Vedānta, and more particularly, within Advaita Vedānta. For sleep (or more accurately 'deep' or 'dreamless sleep') is identified as one of the three states of consciousness. Hence the kind of detailed discussion that this monograph purports to carry out must commence with a description, if only in outline, of the broader schema within which the phenomenon of sleep is lodged in Hindu Vedantic thought.

Any comprehensive system of thought begins by reducing the complexity of the data it must tackle to manageable categories. Physics, for instance, reduces the material world of everyday life, with all its buzzing, blooming confusion, to the categories of matter and energy. Chemistry reduces the various substances it must deal with to a table of elements. In the same spirit, Advaita Vedānta, when faced with the problem of bringing the confusing multiplicity of human experiences within manageable limits in preparation for further analysis, tried to encompass the entire range of human experience within the schema of the three states of consciousness.

Were anyone asked to list all the items in consciousness experienced by him or her, he or she is bound to fail in carrying out so enormous an exercise on account of the sheer richness and diversity of the contents of experience. One could even barely commence such a vast undertaking without faltering. It is, however, possible to circumvent the problem by sidestepping it and claiming instead that, irrespective of the specific contents of our experiences, they are *all* experienced by us in one of three states of consciousness—that of waking (*jāgrat*), dreaming (*svapna*), and deep sleep (*suṣupti*). This classification provides us with a handle, as it were, for grabbing hold of that immense vessel of our rich, varied, and ever-growing experiences. Small wonder then that this classification caught on in Hindu philosophical circles. It is also worth noting that this classification is eminently rational. Although the classification is developed within the body of literature considered revelational in Hinduism, the classification itself is not revelational but rather rational in character, for it does not derive its cogency by an appeal to scriptural authority, but from the support it seems to derive from our experience of life itself. In that sense it may be described as philosophical rather than religious in nature.

IV

The following features of this trichotomy deserve special attention as a propadeutic to the study of consciousness.

(1) From the point of view of everyday life, one tends to accord primacy, if not supremacy, to the waking state, viewing deep sleep as a phase of rest and dreaming as the working out of psychic latencies generated during the state of waking. From the point of Vedantic philosophy, however, such a view would be considered unsatisfactory, as it begs the question. Sleep cannot be merely a period of rest as "even the lazy people get sleep, while the old people [who need more rest] get less sleep at night."[1] Similarly, "dream is not the mere result of the unnatural change of the nervous system because even those who are very frugal in their eating and enjoyments and who are in a healthy state get dreams."[2] Indeed—

> Because both deep sleep and dream keep on coming to us even if we do not want them also and because they come to us quite naturally without being subject to our desire to have them in a particular manner only, we will have to say that they also, like the waking, are

> very essential to us. Therefore, it will be proper to opine that deep sleep and dream are independent states created for some good purpose for our sake alone, instead of considering them as dependent states which cause or create facilities or difficulties or hardships required by the waking state.[3]

(2) It may well be that from the point of view of daily living, the waking state holds the key, but philosophy claims to deal with ultimate reality. Therefore,

> However much in our daily transactions we may be very highly benefited by waking, but if there is an ambition to determine the Ultimate Reality, then it is clear from this that we have to practise, first of all, considering the experiences of all the three states which are our own with a common vision (dispassionately), i.e. *with equal importance given to all the three states which are universally everybody's experiences.*[4]

Furthermore, when the matter is probed, we realise that

> we can never perceive with our waking senses the dream and the deep sleep; if it is so, where is the justification for imagining that those two states occur in this waking world alone? In each dream we perceive a different set of objects which seem to us as a world. Do we ever believe that that world has engulfed within itself the world of this waking state or this waking state itself? No. Day to day we experience many different dreams; do we ever believe that one among the worlds of those dreams exists somewhere even when its respective dream does not exist? Not at all. If it is so, what evidence is there to imagine that the waking world alone can exist independently apart from the waking state?[5]

(3) To the extent that Advaita Vedānta emphasizes the role of 'experience' as a datum for philosophizing, let us:

> . . . investigate or deliberate upon the question—'Through which senses or instruments of knowledge do we know or experience the waking state?'—then we realize that, unlike the objects being known through the senses and the happiness and grief being experienced through the mind, we have no other instruments of knowledge whatsoever for 'the experience or knowledge of the waking state'. Just as we experience our dream and deep sleep directly (i.e. intuitively) without the help of any instruments of knowledge like the senses, the mind, etc., in the same manner we experience the waking directly without the need for any instrument of knowledge. Is it not? This is a very important fact. For, in the other schools of philosophy more importance is given to the instruments of knowledge (like the senses, mind) alone; but in the method of the three states of Consciousness which is followed in Vedanta, this Intuitive experience, which is the substratum for the instruments of knowledge, is itself considered as the highest among all the instruments of knowledge that we possess.[6]

That it to say, our experience of the senses and the mind follows upon our being in a waking state and not vice versa.

(4) It could be objected that there are many other states of consciousness beyond those of waking, dreaming, and deep sleep, such as those of intoxication, insanity, swoon, delirium, somnambulism, etc.[7] All of these, however, can be understood as experiences within one of the three states, whose basic feature is their mutual exclusivity: "the world is included within the state and not in the world the states occur."[8]

(5) It might be claimed that "Observed naturally, all the three states belong to the category or species of '*Avasthā*,' or a state of Consciousness; as dream is caused by the latent impressions of the waking and deep sleep is the rest or respite caused to the body, the senses etc., it can be said that among them there is a temporal as well as a cause-effect kind of relationship. Therefore, to many people the statement that there is no relationship among the states seems to be invalid."[9]

This argument compromises the point regarding the mutual exclusivity of the states. However, in Advaita these connections arise not on account of the interconnectedness of the states, but on account of the same person and the same *antaḥkaraṇa* or internal organ of the person being involved in the states of consciousness.

(6) According to Advaita the three states of consciousness also involve a 'fourth' (*turīya*). This is supposed to be the ultimate and true state which underlies the three.

> Beyond *suṣupti*, both quantitatively and qualitatively different from it, is the bliss of *samādhi* which is called the *turīya* state. Though literally *turīya* means the fourth, it is not to be understood as in any sense numerically different. For example, when speaking of a coin from the first quarter to the last, with the first quarter, we say one quarter of the rupee, with the second we say half of the rupee, with the third quarter we say three quarters of the rupee. But when we come to the last quarter of it, we do not speak in terms of 'quarter'; but we say One or whole Rupee. Even so, the *turīya* is a comprehensive whole and it is not to be expressed in terms of the fourth of the four fractions.[10]

(7) The three states of consciousness involve change, as one state is replaced by another. Change *of* or *in* consciousness can only be perceived, according to Advaita, by something itself not subject to such change, which can bear witness to this change. This Advaita identifies as the true subject, often referred to as the Self, which itself cannot be known in the usual empirical manner, for then it would become an object and cease to be the subject. "The self is never known. It only knows. It illumines all things, including the states of deep sleep, dream and wakefulness."[11] Further analysis discloses that the essence of this self or subject is pure consciousness in the following manner according to Advaita Vedānta:

> If again we compare the three states, namely of waking, dreaming and sleeping without dreams, which

> the human self experiences daily, we can reach the same conception. The essence of the self must remain in all these or the self would cease to be. But what do we find common to all these states? In the first state there is consciousness of external objects; in the second also there is consciousness, but of internal objects present only to the dreamer. In the third state no objects appear, but there is no cessation of consciousness, for otherwise the subsequent memory of that state, as one of peace and freedom from worries, would not be possible. The persistent factor then is consciousness, but not necessarily of any object. This shows again that the essence of self is pure consciousness without necessary relation to object.[12]

V

Sleep becomes an issue in Advaita Vedānta for reasons which are philosophical both generally and in a specifically Advaitic sense.

It is an issue generally because although Advaita claims to treat all the states on par, the fact remains that "just as in the case of empirical transactions, in the *same way in the case of scriptural transactions* also the waking viewpoint is extremely essential"[13] and the issue of the primacy or otherwise of a waking state keeps asserting itself. This general point also possesses an Advaitic dimension, as scriptural authority (*śabda*) is sometimes accorded great significance in the formal articulation of Advaita.

From a specifically Advaitic point of view the experience of sleep poses several problems. For one, in the plenary Advaitic experience the subject-object distinction vanishes. This also happens in sleep, yet sleep is not normally considered identical with the plenary experience. From the point of view of the plenary experience sleep presents another paradox. The plenary experience, wherein the subject-object dichotomy disappears as in sleep, is supposed to consist of happiness par excellence. People upon awakening from sleep also testify to having slept happily. In sleep, however, they are also in a state of ignorance about themselves whereas the plenary Advaitic experience is also said to be one characterised by total awareness rather than utter ignorance.

Thus the fact that both sleep and Realization represent non-dual forms of consciousness and yet the former is not considered soteriological in the same sense as the latter raises tantalizing issues, and generates a debate if the views of Śaṅkara and Gauḍapāda are placed alongside. Thus Śaṅkara arguably claims, at least on occasion, that deep sleep is a form of Brahman experience (on account of the association of sleep with bliss) but his predecessor Gauḍapāda is more inclined to look upon sleep as just another manifestation of *avidyā* or ignorance, (on account of the association of sleep with nonawareness).

This consideration is further complicated by the fact "there is one more significant instance where there is awareness because of the witness"—despite ignorance—"without the instrumentation of the cognitive mode—the awareness of the absence of objects as in deep sleep."[14] This point may be elaborated as follows:

> What really happens when one goes to sleep? There seem to be intermittent periods of lapsing into total unconsciousness. Had there been a break in the flow of consciousness one could not on waking resume the threads of personal identity. On waking up one says "I slept soundly, I didn't know anything". Paradoxically this not knowing of anything is itself known. Consciousness does not remain ignorant of its own ignorance. The sleeping self is thus revealed as revealing the darkness (Ajñāna) which is a kind of loose embodiment for the self, and which is the matrix of all distinctions and differentiations of the waking life. Therefore revelation is absolute and timeless, depending in the adventitious fact of there being something to be revealed. Advaita makes a basic distinction between consciousness and knowledge. Knowledge is the revelation of objects by means of modifications (Vṛttis), while consciousness is the principle of revela-

> tion itself, without their being a principle of revelation the entire world would be plunged in darkness (Jagad Āndhya Prasaṅga).[15]

The relationship of the experience of deep sleep to the experience of *brahman* in a sense constitutes the crux of the matter. Both possess a non-dual character and yet both are distinct. To the extent that the two are indistinguishable sleep can be used to illustrate the experience of Brahman. To the extent that the two, though indistinguishable in some ways are not identical in all respects, some daylight between the two must be allowed. It is within this light that the role of sleep in Advaita Vedānta needs to be investigated.

1

Sleep in Advaita Vedānta: A Prologue

Karl H. Potter, in his introduction to the philosophy of Advaita Vedānta, lists twelve propositions as constituting the theoretical basis of Advaita. The last of these propositions reads as follows: "Pure consciousness is experienced during deep sleep; since we awake refreshed, it is inferred that pure consciousness (reality, Brahman, the true Self) is also the ultimate bliss."[1]

The statement is merely an earnest of the profound role the phenomenon of deep sleep plays in the formulation of the philosophy of Advaita Vedānta. We read in one of its major proof-texts, the *Chāndogyopaniṣad*: "Uddālaka son of Aruṇa said to his son Śvetaketu, 'Learn from me the doctrine of the sleep. When a man literally "sleeps" [*svapiti*], then he has merged with Existent. He has "entered the self" [*svamapītaḥ*], that is why they say that he "sleeps." For he has entered the self.' "[2]

The physiological experience of deep sleep continues to be profoundly significant in the subsequent evolution of Advaita, as well as in its classical formulation at the hands of Śaṅkara. This is a matter of some surprise, as sleep, on the basis of ordinary experience, may be regarded as a state of *un*consciousness, as a time we need to take off from the waking state to return to it with renewed vigor in the pursuit of our normal, or even intellectual and philosophical, pursuits. This rather surprising role the phenomenon of deep sleep plays in Advaita has led William M. Indich to remark:

> This phenomenological analysis of the deep sleep state is extremely important for the Advaitin, for it is in terms of this analysis that he argues for the non-dual, self-luminous and, . . . the blissful nature of pure consciousness. It may seem somewhat odd to a person trained in Western philosophy that an analysis of dreamless sleep should play a significant role in the philosophical defense of a particular theory of consciousness. Of course, both Freud and Jung saw in sleep a physiologically and psychologically necessary period of relief and recovery from the strains of waking experience, a point that goes back at least as far as Aristotle, but there seems to be little of philosophical concern for these thinkers behind this observation. On the other hand, while Śaṅkara discusses the physiology of sleep and acknowledges its value in allowing the individual to recover from fatigue, he goes beyond this and extracts arguments for his theory of Self from his discussion of sleep. And he is not alone among Indian philosophers in doing this.[3]

This then is the paradox to be confronted: that a state of being normally associated with unconsciousness becomes, in the hands of the Advaitins, the cornerstone of their doctrine of pure consciousness, a doctrine that constitutes the basis of the philosophical system. A striking illustration of this is found in the vantage point accorded to different states of consciousness in normal living and in Advaita. In normal living the baseline is provided by the *waking state*.[4] From this waking state we pass into sleep—either a state of dreaming or deep sleep. In Advaita the perspective is reversed. The state of *deep sleep*

> is said to be the gateway to cognition (*cetomukha*). From a blissful non-awareness of things and events in sleep,

> one either wakes up gradually and eventually to full consciousness of the external world, or passes to the experience of objects and events in a dream. On the one hand, one goes into dreamless sleep from waking and dream, and on the other, one lapses from sleep into either of these states. Hence it is called the gateway of consciousness, alike to its entrance and to its exit.[5]

It might be useful to state here, in a general way, the metaphysical status of deep sleep in Advaita Vedānta, as we proceed to examine its role in particular texts and thinkers. The following account meets this need well:

> Deep sleep (*suṣupta*) is the self in the form of *prājña,* an undifferentiated and self-luminous mass of consciousness. Here one is desireless, without the superimposition of gross *or* subtle limitations. One rests in pure self-awareness, full of bliss (*ānanda*). Sleep is the source and limit of the other states, and most like the self in its true nature. Still, one inevitably returns from sleep to waking limitations, and the sleeper is ignorant within the bliss.[6]

2

Sleep in the *Prasthānatraya* (Upaniṣads, Brahmasūtra, Bhagavadgītā)

I

The tradition of Advaita Vedānta can certainly be traced as far back as the *Bṛhadāraṇyaka* and *Chāndogya Upaniṣads*, the two earliest Upaniṣads.[1] They are also considered primarily absolutistic in character. In both of them the analysis of the human condition involves the analysis of deep sleep. It will be useful to compare and contrast these analyses. With this end in view, the analysis of sleep carried out in each is presented in the context of the search for the true self of a human being as depicted in these two Upaniṣads.

In the *Chāndogya Upaniṣad*, Prajāpati:

> teaches first that the self is the body, but this is clearly inadequate; the self then would suffer all the changes of the body. Prajāpati teaches next that the self is "he who moves about happy in a dream"; but the dream self experiences not only happiness but also unpleasantness and pain. Then, it is said, the self is when a man is asleep, composed, serene, knows no dream. But in that state there is no awareness even of personal

> existence; such a one "has gone to annihilation" (*Chāndogya Upaniṣad* 8.11.1).
>
> Prajāpati then offers a final explanation: the body, which is mortal, is only the support of the deathless, bodiless self. Freed from the body, the self rises up and reaches the highest life, where it appears in his own form as "the supreme person". There it moves about, laughing, playing, and rejoicing, without remembering the appendage of the body. "As an animal is attached to a cart, so is life attached to this body". It is the sense organs that see, smell, utter sound, hear, and think: the self perceives, but is not attached to the organs of perception (*Chāndogya* 8.12, 4–5).[2]

In the *Bṛhadāraṇyaka*, Yājñavalkya works his way through the human psychological processes in the search for the self, and after discussing the two states of waking and dreaming, he presents an analysis of dreamless sleep.

> In a third state, that of "deep sleep", the self is free even from the appearance of activity. In both the waking and dream states it might be thought through ignorance that the self is affected by what happens to the forms or to the body; thus there is pain, fears, and craving. In the state of deep sleep, however, these apparent attachments are removed and the self is seen in its true condition of freedom.[2A]

> This verily is his form which is free from craving, free from evils, free from fear. As a man when in the embrace of his beloved wife knows nothing without or within, so the person when in the embrace of the intelligent self knows nothing without or within. That verily is his form in which his desire is fulfilled, in which the self is his desire, in which he is without desire, free from any sorrow. (*Bṛhadāraṇyaka* 4.3.21)[3]

This is not a state of unconsciousness, but, as the analogy with sexual intercourse indicates, a state of totally unified consciousness in which there is no awareness of difference. The self in this condition maintains its character as a perceiver, but there is nothing else separate from it that it could perceive. In this state, free of all fear and desire, and conscious only of oneness, the self experiences the highest bliss, *ānanda*, the bliss of the world of Brahman. But this state is not attained permanently in deep sleep, and there is an inevitable return to the states of dream and waking. The state of deep sleep is only a precursor of the desired permanent condition of release.

Yājñavalkya then goes on to describe the self at the time of death and the final attainment of Brahman.

> Here, as in sleep, speculation is tied to observation. When a person approaches death, his senses cease to function properly. They are withdrawn from the outside world, gathered in, so that one by one the person loses external sense contact. With the senses withdrawn, the unified self departs from the body and the senses or life breaths depart with it.[4]

It becomes clear from a comparison of the two Upaniṣads that although there are similarities in their analysis of the human condition, there are also differences in their portrayal of this condition. Some of these also extend to the treatment of deep sleep. But these differences are connected with the difference in their overall view about human destiny.

> . . . In Yājñavalkya's view, there is no merger with Brahman except for the released self, and then the merger is permanent. The transmigratory self remains separate from Brahman, still bound to phenomenal existence by the influence of past actions carried along with the self.
>
> . . . In Yājñavalkya's teaching the vital powers are directly involved in bodily activity and carry the effects of that attachment with them in the "knowledge and past deeds and memory" that take hold of the subtle self. No such positive influence is evident in

> Uddālaka's statements, and actions as such seem a less important factor in rebirth. The emphasis is instead more directly on the absence of knowledge. All bodily manifestations devolve back into the Real at the time of death, but the merger is not complete unless there is prior knowledge of the Real. Only a person who knows that Brahman is his own reality remains in the condition of union, since only his knowledge is sufficiently purified of all false understanding. Only such a person has no doubts, and can enter the merger with the One with assurance that this is his final resting place.[5]

It is clear that the reemergence of a human being, after having enjoyed deep sleep but without becoming liberated in the process, poses a challenge in both the Upaniṣads but in slightly different ways. In the *Bṛhadāraṇyaka Upaniṣad* the problem arises because of the striking similarities between the *states* of deep sleep and liberation. Consider for instance the following passages. The first describes the state of self in deep sleep (IV.3.31). "31. Verily, when there is, as it were, another there one might see the other, one might smell the other, one might taste the other, one might speak to the other, one might hear the other, one might think of the other, one might touch the other, one might know the other."[6]

This second passage pertains to a state of liberation (II.4.14):

> 14. 'For where there is duality as it were, there one smells another, there one sees another, there one hears another, there one speaks to another, there one thinks of another, there one understands another. Where, verily, everything has become the Self, then by what and whom should one smell, then by what and whom should one see, then by what and whom should one hear, then by what and to whom should one speak, then by what and on whom should one think, then by what and whom should one understand? By what

> should one know that by which all this is known? By what, my dear, should one know the knower?'[7]

In the case of *Chāndogya*, because of its, shall we say, cyclical view of absorption and emergence of human beings from Brahman, in contrast to the linear view of human beings being progressively reborn till release is attained, the difficulties seem to arise from the fact that one in some sense merges into Brahman in deep sleep, and hence the issue of re-emergence comes to the fore. The issue in the *Bṛhadāraṇyaka* has soteriological overtones. In the *Chāndogya* it possesses ontological overtones. *Chāndogya* VIII.3.2 reads:

> 2. But those of one's (fellows) whether they are alive or whether they have departed and whatever else one desires but does not get, all this one finds by going in there (into one's own self); for here, indeed, are those true desires of his with a covering of what is false. Just as those who do not know the field walk again and again over the hidden treasure of gold and do not find it, even so all creatures here go day after day into the Brahma-world and yet do not find it, for they are carried away by untruth.[8]

The reference to a daily visit to the Brahma-world is widely acknowledged as a reference to sleep.[9] The issue of the comparison of sleep in the two Upaniṣads may now be pressed a little further.

> There are some similarities between the BāU and the ChU accounts. Both teach that the *puruṣa/ātman*, free from sorrow or flaw, is the basis of changing states. They also concur that dreams are less conditioned than waking, and that deep sleep is free from any limitations at all. However the BāU's serenely restful sleep becomes "going to destruction" in the ChU. The BāU explicitly says that the self in sleep possesses indestructibility (*avināśitva*), although it sees no other (BāU

> IV.3.23.). "Seeing no other" suggests to Indra that one *is* gone to destruction.
>
> . . . Whereas the non-duality of deep sleep and the bliss of self-knowledge are one in the BāU, they are clearly separated in the *Chāndogya*. Something more positive than "mere" non-duality is desired in the ChU; deep sleep is pure, but also seems ignorant of the highest reality. As we shall see, later advaitins diverge on the BāU and ChU interpretations.[10]

This does not take long. "Gauḍapāda (with the ChU) holds that sleep primarily indicates ignorance; Śaṅkara (with the BāU and the MāU) emphasizes the bliss aspect. None, however, disputes the idea that sleep has a special status, in some way closer to the eternal flawless self than waking and dream."[11]

One salient fact stands out for special notice in the discussion of deep sleep in Advaita in the earliest Upaniṣads, namely, that finally the state of deep sleep is *identified neither with annihilation nor liberation*. There is a stage in the progressive teaching in the *Chāndogya* (VIII.11.2–3) when a tentative identification with annihilation does occur, but even there it constitutes only one of the two interpretations of sleep; it is the identification of the *self* with deep sleep that is objected to as indicative of an unsatisfactory concept of the self:

> 1. When a man is asleep, composed, serene, and knows no dream, that is the self, said he, that is the immortal, the fearless. That is Brahman. Then he went forth with tranquil heart. Even before reaching the gods he saw this danger. In truth this one does not know himself that 'I am he', nor indeed the things here. He has become one who has gone to annihilation. I see no good in this.
>
> 2. He came back again with fuel in hand to him. *Prajāpati* said, 'Desiring what, O Maghavan, have you come back, since you went away with a tranquil heart?' Then he said, 'Venerable Sir, in truth this one does not know

himself that I am he, nor indeed the things here. He has become one who has gone to annihilation. I see no good in this'.[12]

In the *Bṛhadāraṇyaka Upaniṣad*, when the nondual nature of deep sleep is explained by Yājñavalkya to Janaka, Janaka does not object to his description, part of which is cited below.

27. 'Verily, when there (in the state of deep sleep) he does not hear, he is, verily, hearing, though he does not hear, for there is no cessation of the hearing of a hearer, because of the imperishability (of the hearer). There is not, however, a second, nothing else separate from him which he could hear.

28. 'Verily, when there (in the state of deep sleep) he does not think, he is, verily, thinking, though he does not think, for there is no cessation of the thinking of a thinker, because of the imperishability (of the thinker). There is not, however, a second, nothing else separate from him of which he could think.

29. 'Verily, when there (in the state of deep sleep) he does not touch, he is, verily, touching, though he does not touch, for there is no cessation of the touching of a toucher, because of the imperishability (of the toucher). There is not, however, a second, nothing else separate from him which he could touch.

30. 'Verily, when there (in the state of deep sleep) he does not know, he is, verily, knowing though he does not know for there is no cessation of the knowing of a knower, because of the imperishability (of the knower). There is not, however, a second, nothing else separate from him which he could know.

31. 'Verily, when there is, as it were, another there one might see the other, one might smell the other, one might taste the other, one might speak to the other,

> one might hear the other, one might think of the other, one might touch the other, one might know the other.[13]

The existence of a knower is never questioned, nor the *fact of consciousness,* although consciousness cannot manifest itself as the consciousness of another. In the description of nondual liberation *however,* when Yājñavalkya tells his beloved wife Maitreyī in the *Bṛhadāraṇyaka Upaniṣad* (IV.5.14) that in the liberated state there is *no consciousness,* she is bewildered.

> 13. As a mass of salt is without inside, without outside, is altogether, a mass of taste, even so, verily, is this Self without inside, without outside, altogether a mass of intelligence only. Having arisen out of these elements (the Self) vanishes again in them. When he has departed there is no more (separate or particular) consciousness. Thus, verily, say 'I', said Yājñavalkya. Particular consciousness is due to association with elements; when this association is dissolved through knowledge, knowledge of oneness is obtained and particular consciousness disappears.
>
> 14. Then Maitreyī said: 'Here, indeed, Venerable Sir, you have caused me to reach utter bewilderment. Indeed, I do not at all understand this (the Self)'. He replied, 'I do not say anything bewildering. This Self, verily, is imperishable and of indestructible nature.'[14]

Two further points deserve to be specially noted in relation to sleep in the *Bṛhadāraṇyaka Upaniṣad.* Although we have focused primarily on Yājñavalkya's understanding of the phenomenon of sleep, it contains another account that in some ways is closer to the *Chāndogya.* It may be described as constituting Ajātaśatru's understanding of the nature of deep sleep, as distinguished from Yājñavalkya's. In *Bṛhadāraṇyaka* .1.16–19:

> Ajātaśatru asks Gārgya where the person (*puruṣa,* the internal vital force) who consists of awareness (*vijñānamaya*) goes when sleeping. Gārgya does not know, so

Ajātaśatru explains that when sleeping, the person withdraws his sense-functions and rests in the space within the heart. When the senses are indrawn, so are the vital breath (*prāṇa*) and mental activity.

Then Ajātaśatru describes how the *puruṣa* moves in dream with his senses indrawn. He becomes like a brahmin or a great king who goes around his own country as he pleases. Just like this, the *puruṣa* (with his senses) goes around in the body as he pleases. When the person reaches deep sleep (*suṣupta*), he knows nothing and moves through internal channels (*hita*), coming to rest near the heart. He rests as the great king or brahmin would, having reached the extreme "oblivion" (*atighnī*) of bliss.

In this account of dream and deep sleep, we first find the senses indrawn and the *puruṣa* moving around in the body. Then there is deep rest and no knowledge at all. It is important to note that this "oblivion" is equated with bliss, rather than dullness or mere quiescence.[15]

By way of contrast, and this is the second point:

Yājñavalkya describes the *puruṣa*'s end as without fear or flaw and beyond desire. Embraced by the fully conscious self (*prajñāna ātman*), the *puruṣa* knows nothing inside or out (or perhaps perceives nothing while "knowing" all). The embrace of the self ends all sorrow and want. As we shall see, the *puruṣa*'s condition now is much like later descriptions of the self in sleep: desireless, dreamless, and knowing nothing. This quiescence is bliss.

The passage concludes by discussing the nature of the *puruṣa*'s "seeing." While not seeing as one does in waking state, the *puruṣa* "sees" eternally. This higher seeing could not be destroyed (*avināśi*), and is without a second; there is no other to be seen (smelled, heard, or discriminated, etc.). Sensing another is not possible for the seer (*draṣṭṛ*) is one non-dual "ocean." Reaching this end is the highest goal (path, world), and greatest

> bliss. Thus, this "eternal seeing" is a possible starting point for the concept of *turīya.*[16]

The *turīya* state is the fourth state, constituting liberation, beyond the three states of waking, dreaming and deep sleep.

The point is important: "*Jñāna* does not vary even in deep sleep: the knowing of the knower is never destroyed."[17]

Three other Upaniṣads, assigned to a period after the *Bṛhadāraṇyaka* and the *Chāndogya,* may now be examined for the light they shed on the question of sleep, namely, the *Praśna, Kauṣītakī,* and *Maitrī Upaniṣads.* In the *Praśna Upaniṣad,* the close association of sleep with bliss and the Supreme Self is stated as follows (IV.6.7.9–11):

> When he is overcome with light, then in this state, the god (mind) sees no dreams. Then here in his body arises this happiness.
>
> Even as birds, O dear, resort to a tree for a resting-place, so does everything here resort to the Supreme Self. They all find their rest in the Supreme Self.
>
> He, verily, is the seer, the toucher, the hearer, the smeller, the taster, the perceiver, the knower, the doer, the thinking self, the person. He becomes established in the Supreme Undecaying Self.
>
> He who knows the shadowless, bodiless, colourless, pure, undecaying self attains verily, the Supreme, Undecaying (self). He who, O dear, knows thus becomes omniscient, (becomes) all. As to this, there is this verse: He who knows that Undecaying (self) in which are established the self of the nature of intelligence, the vital breaths and the elements along with all the gods (powers) becomes, O dear, omniscient and enters all.[18]

By contrast, in the *Kauṣītakī* the *prājña ātman* is mentioned and "*Kauṣītaki* III.3 equates the *prājña ātman* with the *prāṇa* and says that in deep sleep a person becomes one with *prāṇa.*"[19]

The pattern of relationships that finally gains consensus in Advaita differs somewhat from these and finds a clear enunciation in the *Maitrī Upaniṣad*.

> He who sees with the eye, who moves in dreams, who is sound asleep and he who is beyond the sound sleeper, these are a person's four distinct conditions. Of these the fourth is greater than the rest. *Brahman* with one quarter moves in the three and with three-quarters in the last. For the sake of experiencing the true and the false the great self has a dual nature, yea, the great self has a dual nature.[20]

Andrew Fort remarks on this passage as follows:

> Reference to *Ṛgveda* X.90 is unmistakable here, but the Vedic scheme is reversed. The RV's one quarter of brahman which is the sphere of all beings here becomes three states, while the RV's three divine quarters are included within the *Maitri's turīya*. Thus, proportions are inverted, and emphasis is laid on consciousness states, particularly the one which is beyond and greater than the other three. The Upaniṣad's final line then indicates that the three-in-one and on-in-three reveal the self's dual nature: one *and* many.
>
> The primary motive seems to be to "update" the Vedic *catuṣpāda* scheme with more recent conceptions of a non-dual and blissful self underlying ever-changing states, while at the same time giving this new conception Vedic sanction. We also notice an implicit answer to Indra in ChU VIII: there is a fourth "state" beyond and greater than deep sleep. Other than containing three quarters of brahman, this fourth remains uncharacterized (and later is said to be uncharaterizable).[21]

Deep sleep finds a clearly established and distinguished place in the *catuṣpāda* doctrine, as enunciated in the *Māṇḍūkya Upaniṣad*, to be discussed later. The scheme in *Maitrī* closely resembles the one found in *Māṇḍūkya*. The key point to note in all this is that "there are no references to the MāU or to the *catuṣpāda* doctrine, in the *Brahmasūtra* or in the *Bhagavadgītā*."[22] The last two, along with the Upaniṣads, constitute the triple canon of Advaita Vedānta. Hence the significance of the present discussion regarding the location of deep sleep in the *catuṣpāda* doctrine, of which the *Māṇḍūkya Upaniṣad* is said to provide the most systematic formulation.

> The *Māṇḍūkya's* description of the states of consciousness shows continuity with earlier Upaniṣadic conceptions. The waking sphere is limited to cognizing gross and external things. Dreaming is a little closer to self-knowledge, for one then cognizes subtle and internal things. Waking and dreaming are structurally similar however—a point which Gauḍapāda takes pains to elaborate (GK II.1–15).
>
> The structural similarity of the first two quarters breaks down in the sleep sphere. As in earlier texts, sleep is linked with bliss and unified consciousness. It is clearly the most enjoyable and worthy of attaining. The self now becomes the omniscient ruler, the inner controller, and the one womb of all. Sleep's auspicious qualities here are far different from a conception of sleep as dullness and mere lack of awareness.
>
> Finally, the fourth goes far beyond the first three quarters. A series of negations is the only appropriate description. The fourth is the ground of existence and awareness but, in the M U, this does not entail positive attributes—they are left behind in deep sleep. One wonders whether or not Indra (ChU VIII) would find any satisfaction here either.[23]

There is general agreement among the Upaniṣads such as *Bṛhadāraṇyaka*, *Chāndogya*, *Praśna* (IV.6), *Kauṣītakī* (III.8), etc., that, so far as deep sleep itself is concerned, there are within it no distinctions whatever of knowing subject and known object, and one is not conscious of what is without, or what is within. In fact the very notions of 'without' and 'within' have no meaning when all empirical distinctions vanish in the state of sleep. This is what is meant when it is said that in sleep there is loss of objective consciousness. Thus it is generally agreed that, in deep sleep, "there is no duality. There is one undivided consciousness which is of the nature of bliss."[24]

On the basis of the experience of deep sleep, however, Advaita also draws certain conclusions about the nature of the self. It may be possible to agree with the description or even the assessment of the experience of deep sleep qua experience as it is presented in Advaita—but there is room for difference of opinion when Advaita "speculates" about the nature of the self on the basis of this experience, as when it is claimed that "the sleeper attains temporary union with the . . . pure witness-self";[25] or that in sleep the "*self* is beyond desires, free from evil, and fearless."[26] The one who sleeps shares in these features of deep sleep but the attribution of these to the "self" raises the question whether the attribution of the features of sleep to the self is legitimate. Similarly, it is claimed that in the state of deep sleep "the self is realized to be relationless . . . In that state the self sees and yet does not see. There is no seeing of objects, but *sight* remains. The 'sight' of the seer is never lost because it is imperishable. Just as the presence of the objects is revealed by the self, their absence too is revealed by it."[27] It is further claimed that "Consciousness *per se* neither rises nor sets. It is self-luminous. *That the self is non-dual consciousness is evident from the experience of sleep*. There is then no other besides it which it could see."[28] Whether such deductions about the nature of self from the nature of deep sleep are valid remains a moot point.

A further specifically Advaitin association is made in *Māṇḍūkya* 6 about the self in deep sleep, namely, that "This is the lord of all, this is the knower of all, this is the inner controller; this is the source of all; this is the beginning and the end of being."[29]

The words used: *sarveśvara, sarvajña, antaryāmī* are the names used for God or Īśvara in Hindu thought. Thus herein a cosmic identification seems to have been made, just a step removed from the *ātman* = Brahman identity. As the self in deep sleep is called *prājña*, one might call this the *prājña* = *Īśvara* identification.

I think the Upaniṣads perform a great service in drawing philosophical attention to the *uniqueness* of the experience of deep sleep. In a way each state—*waking, dreaming* as well as *deep sleep*—is unique; but deep sleep falls in a class apart, as it calls the subject-object distinction experientially into question. It is unique and yet a universal experience. Without it one would be hard put to establish the credibility of a state of consciousness of which one is not conscious while in it. However, some of the conclusions drawn on the basis of the experience of deep sleep need to be critically examined.

(1) The tendency to identify the state of nonduality in deep sleep with that of non-dual Realization is worth remarking. There is an occasional tendency to do so, even in the Upaniṣads, as in *Chāndogya* VI.8.2 also cited earlier: "Then Uddālaka Āruṇi said to his son, Śvetaketu, learn from me, my dear, the true nature of sleep. When a person here sleeps, as it is called, then, my dear, he has reached pure being. He has gone to his own. Therefore they say he sleeps for he has gone to his own."[30] Modern scholarship is also not immune from this tendency. For instance, M. Hiriyanna, while presenting the role of reason in Advaita Vedānta, declares: "The Upanishads themselves declare that when a person has seen this truth for himself, he outgrows the need for the scriptures. 'There a father becomes no father; a mother, no mother; the world, no world; the gods, no gods; the Vedas, no Vedas.' "[31] He is cautious to note, after acknowledging the source as *Bṛhadāraṇyaka Upaniṣad* IV.iii.22 that "this passage, no doubt, refers to deep sleep"; but adds that "*mokṣa* is, in this respect, only a replica of deep sleep."[32] K. Satchidananda Murty writes: "Śaṅkara unhesitatingly states that when the final truth of non-dualism is realized, there will be no perception; for the Veda also would become non-existent then."[33] Murty cites Śaṅkara's gloss on *Brahmasūtra* IV.1.3 in support as did Hiriyanna, but he *also* adds in support *Bṛhadāraṇyaka* IV.3.33: *yatra vedā avedāḥ* without clarifying that the context here is one of deep sleep and not realization.[34] Even Śaṅkara himself, it seems, has applied this expression to the state of enlightenment.[35] He may be justified in doing so, but this complicates

the issue when one is trying to distinguish between deep sleep and enlightenment.

(2) It is claimed on the *basis of experience* of deep sleep that consciousness is self-luminous. But Citsukha, an Advaitin of the thirteenth century and author of *Tattvapradīpikā*, defines self-luminosity as "the capacity of being called immediately known in *empirical* usage while not being an object of cognition."[36] In deep sleep there is no object of cognition. Hence, in *this* sense, the state of deep sleep, one could claim, would not correspond to empirical usage. Nor is the state immediately known, in the conventional sense, as there is no knowledge of it as such at the time. All this raises grave doubts about the claim of self-luminosity in relation to deep sleep, despite the assertion in Vidyāraṇya's *Pañcadaśī* that it illustrates "the self-revealing nature of the non-dual."[37] It is certainly not self-revealing in the usual sense. This point regarding the self-luminosity as defined earlier should be carefully distinguished from the claim that consciousness in some way or another characterises all the three states of waking, dreaming, and dreamless sleep.

> In different ways the Advaitin establishes the supreme reality of a transcendental principle of pure consciousness, which, though always untouched and unattached in its own nature, is yet the underlying principle which can explain all the facts of our experience. Vidyāraṇya in his *Pañca-daśī* states that there is no moment when there is no consciousness whether in our awakened states or dreams or in our dreamless condition. Even in dreamless sleep there is consciousness for later we remember the experience of the dreamless state.[38]

This claim, however, is of another kind and not on all fours with the one made earlier.

(3) It has been claimed that the state of the self in dreamless sleep is that of the pure subject, that of *sākṣī*.[39] Some may regard it as a state in which a subject exists per se but without an object, perhaps on the basis of passages from the *Bṛhadāraṇyaka* cited

earlier. But the experience of deep sleep rather seems to indicate the disappearance of *both* the subject and the object. In this context the following remarks by M. Hiriyanna help consolidate the earlier observations and confirm the present one:

> In this state, described as suṣupti, the manas as well as the senses is quiescent and there is consequently a cessation of normal or empirical consciousness. There is no longer any contrasting of one object with another or even of the subject with the object, and the embodied self is then said to attain a temporary union with the Absolute. As however suṣupti is not identified with the state of release, this statement has to be understood negatively—as only signifying that the consciousness of individuality is absent at the time though the individual himself continues to be, as shown by the sense of personal identity connecting the states before and after sleep. It is not a state of blank or absolute unconsciousness either, for some sort of awareness is associated with it. *It is not, however, the 'objectless knowing subject' that endures in it, as it is sometimes stated; for along with the object, the subject also as such disappears then.* It is rather a state of non-reflective awareness, if we may so term it. This state is above all desire and is therefore described as one of unalloyed bliss.[40]

It may be useful to draw a parallel here between sleep and *samādhi* and to indicate that those who admit to an 'objectless knowing subject' in deep sleep are in a sense talking of *savikalpa suṣupti* (or deep sleep), and those who maintain that both subject and object disappear in deep sleep are talking about *nir-vikalpa suṣupti* in the light of the following passage.

> The Self is experienced as the Absolute Reality in the state of turīya. It is raised above the distinction of subject and object. In suṣupti or deep sleep, the empirical mind with all its modes is inactive. In sa-vikalpa samādhi the mind is concentrated on one object with

which it becomes identified. In it we have the consciousness of determinate reality. The consciousness of duality is absent in this state and the self enjoys undifferenced bliss. In both these states the seeds of knowledge and action, vidyā and karma, are present. In nir-vikalpa samādhi we have the intuition of reality transcending all determinations. This is the highest stage, the truth, Brahman.[41]

(4) The identification of *prājña*, or the self in deep sleep, with Īśvara, seems to be problematical. The problem arises from the fact that obscuration or *āvaraṇa* is the basic feature of deep sleep. Indeed, one way of distinguishing it from waking-cum-dreaming is to say that in their case *vikeṣpa* has also become operational—*āvaraṇa* and *vikṣepa* being associated with *māyā* as its two *śaktis* or powers. Now "it should be remembered that in his *sūtrabhāṣya* Śaṅkara has said that God alone is free from *āvaraṇa dośa* (the defect of 'obscuration' of the intellect), while individuals are not."[42] If this be so, then there is a major reservation that must be kept in mind if *prājña* is equated with Īśvara. The distinction between Īśvara and *jīva* in this respect is explained at some length by Śaṅkara in his commentary on the Thirteenth Chapter of the *Bhagavadgītā*.

> 'Now as to the objections that Īśvara would be a saṁsārin if He be one with Kshetrajña, and that if Kshetrajñas be one with Īśvara there can be no saṁsāra because there is no saṁsārin: these objections have been met by saying that knowledge and ignorance are distinct in kind and in effects, as admitted by all—To explain: The Real Entity (viz., Īśvara) is not affected by the defect (saṁsāra) attributed to Him through ignorance of that Real Entity. This has also been illustrated by the fact that the water of the mirage does not wet the saline soil. And the objection raised on the ground that in the absence of a saṁsārin there can be no saṁsāra has been answered by explaining that the saṁsāra and the saṁsārin are creatures of avidyā.

> (Objection):—The very fact that Kshetrajña is possessed of avidyā makes Him a saṁsārin; and the effect thereof—unhappiness and misery and so on—is directly perceived.
>
> (Answer): No; for, what is perceived is an attribute of Kshetra (matter); and Kshetrajña, the cogniser, cannot be vitiated by the blemish—not inhering in Kshetrajña—you ascribe to Him, it comes under the cognised, and therefore forms a property of Kshetra, and not a property of Kshetrajña. Nor is Kshetrajña affected by it, since such intimate association of the cogniser and the cognised is impossible. If there should be such an association, then that blemish could not be cognised. That is to say, if misery and nescience were properties of the Self, how could they be objects of immediate perception? Or, how could they ever by regarded as the properties of the Self? Since it has been determined that all that is knowable is Kshetra (xiii.5–6), and that Kshetrajña is the knower and none else (xiii.1), it is nothing but sheer ignorance which may lead one to contradict it by saying that nescience and misery and the like are the attributes and specific properties of Kshetrajña and that they are immediately perceived as such.'[43]

It could still be argued that since, according to one interpretation of *tat tvam asi, jīva* can be equated with Īśvara, there should be no hesitation in equating *prājña* with Īśvara. To examine this point let us follow the logic by which *jīva* is equated with Īśvara when *tattvamasi* is interpreted in this light.

> The finite adjunct of the individual self is sometimes designated as *avidyā* to contrast it with the cosmic Maya of the qualified Brahman. In this view, Maya is the whole of which the many *avidyās*, associated with the individual selves, are parts or phases. Just as the whole universe is the effect of Maya, the portions of the universe which constitute the accompaniments of an

> individual self, like the physical body and the internal organ, are regarded as derived from the *avidyā* of that particular self. Whatever distinction there appears to be between the ego and the qualified Brahman or between one ego and another, is entirely due to these differing adjuncts. In themselves, the egos are not distinct from one another or from the qualified Brahman. This identity of denotation of the two terms, *jīva* and the qualified Brahman, while their connotations are different, is the Advaitic interpretation of "That thou art" (*Tat tvam asi*). It does not mean, as it is so often represented to do, that man and the qualified Brahman or God (to use a term which we shall soon explain) are as such one. Such an attitude is as blasphemous, according to Advaita, as it is according to any religion or purely theistic doctrine.[44]

The equation of *prājña* with Īśvara will have to steer clear of the last pitfall. If *jīva* without adjuncts equals Brahman without adjuncts, then *jīva* in *any* state—waking, dreaming, or deep sleep—could be equated with Īśvara while implicated in all of these states.

II

The *Brahmasūtra*, the Upaniṣads, and the *Bhagavadgītā*, constitute the triple foundation of Vedānta.[45] One may therefore turn next to the *Brahmasūtra* for its teachings regarding deep sleep.

The part of the *Brahmasūtra* that concerns us is the one which deals with the soul as intelligence. It is claimed, in aphorism III.3.18, that the soul is of the nature of intelligence. This invites the immediate objection that as "the soul does not remain intelligent in the states of sleep, swoon, and we say when we wake up from sleep that we are not conscious of anything, it is clear that intelligence is intermittent and so adventitious only."[46] The Advaitin answer to this question runs along the following lines:

> Even in sleep persons have intelligence. For if intelligence were non-existent in sleep, the individual could not say that he did not know anything in deep sleep. The absence of objects is mistaken for the absence of intelligence even as the light pervading space is not apparent owing to the absence of things to be illuminated and not to the absence of its own nature."[47]

In the discussion of aphorisms II.3.30–31 in this section a very important point emerges—an issue that had surfaced in the discussion of the Upaniṣadic material earlier. In order to grasp its full significance the concept of *antaḥkaraṇa* in Advaita physiology and psychology needs to be understood. It broadly corresponds to the idea of the mind and the various functions it performs. It is often translated as the internal organ. Its role in the overall context is explained in the comment by Radhakrishnan on I.3.32 as follows:

> If the internal organ (antaḥ-karaṇa) of which the intellect is a mode is not accepted, then as the senses are always in contact with their objects, there would result the perception of every thing as the requisites of the soul, the senses and objects are present. If this is denied, then there can be no knowledge and nothing would ever be known. The opponent will have to accept the limitation of either the soul or the senses. The self is changeless. The power of the senses which is not impeded either in the previous moment or in the subsequent moment cannot be limited in the middle. We have therefore to accept an internal organ through whose connection and disconnection, perception and non-perception result. We find texts which say: 'I am absent-minded. I did not hear it'. B.U.I.5.3. *So there is an internal organ of which intellect is a mode and it is the connection of the self with this that causes individuation in saṁsāra.*[48]

Now one is in a position to revert to earlier aphorism, that if the soul and intellect are distinct entities they could separate. This is countered by aphorism II.3.30. It is clear from the Upaniṣads that their conjunction "lasts as long as the soul continues to be an individual and [until] its ignorance is not destroyed by the realisation of knowledge. This is evident from the Scriptures."[49]

It could, however, be argued that no such connection is manifest in deep sleep. To this, II.3.31 provides an answer: that it exists *potentially* in that state of deep sleep just as virility or adulthood is *potentially* present in the state of childhood:

> If the objection is raised that in suṣupti, or deep sleep, there is no connection with the intellect (see C.U.VI.8.1) and so it is wrong to say that the connection lasts as long as the individualised state exists, the answer is given in this *sūtra* that even in the state of deep sleep the connection exists in a potential form. Were it not so, it could not have become manifest in the awakened state. See B.U.VI.8.2 and 3. Virility becomes manifest in youth because it exists in a potential condition in the child.[50]

It must be borne in mind that while *individuality ceases in sleep, the individual does not*, and that *while the intellect becomes latent, the Self remains patent*, in the sense that some form of awareness must be presumed to continue in deep sleep, otherwise one could not subsequently be aware that one was unaware in deep sleep.

III

The *Bhagavadgītā* does not directly refer to deep sleep, but it does contain allusions to elements associated with it. For instance, in X.20 Arjuna is addressed as *guḍākeśa*, as also earlier in I.24. W. D. P. Hill observes, regarding this epithet, that "ancient commentators derive the name from *guḍāka* and īśa—'lord of sleep.' But the former word is obscure, and in any case there seems to be no good reason for applying such an epithet to Arjuna. A suggested derivation is from *guḍā* and *keśa*."[51] A lexicographical investigation produces interesting results. Monier Monier-Williams cites the word as *guḍāka* and considers it "a word formed for the etymology of *guḍā-keśa*,"[52] while V. S. Apte provides two meanings of *guḍāka*: (1) sloth and (2) sleep, *without* connecting it with the word *guḍākeśa*, which is subsequently cited but which is taken to mean "thick-haired" and noted as an epithet of both Arjuna and Śiva.[53] Interestingly, Śaṅkara provides two interpretations of the word in his gloss on X.20: (1) one who has conquered sleep or (2) thick-haired, and Hill remarks that Śaṅkara "here gives an alternative explanation (*ghanakeśa*) which modern scholarship approves."[54]

In terms of traditional explanation, then, the word should be taken as *guḍāka*, and although obscure, it does make sense in two ways. If *guḍāka* is taken to mean sloth, it would allude to the physical agility of Arjuna; and if taken to mean sleep, and *sleep is taken to mean ignorance*, then it would compliment Arjuna on his mental alertness. In either case, however, it does not do much to improve our understanding of the nature of deep sleep in Advaita Vedānta.

There is one verse in the *Gītā*, however, which may be said to advance it, through Śaṅkara's commentary on it. It is cited below:

> II.69. **What is night to all beings, therein the self-controlled one is awake. Where all beings are awake, that is the night of the sage who sees.**
>
> To all beings the Supreme Reality is night. Night is by nature tamasic, and, as such, causes confusion of things. The Reality is accessible only to a man of steady knowledge. Just as what is day to others becomes night to night-wanderers, so, to all beings, who are ignorant and who correspond to the night-wanderers, the Supreme Reality is dark, is like night; for it is not accessible to those whose minds are not in It. With reference to that Supreme Reality, the self-restrained Yogin who has subdued the senses, and who has shaken off the sleep of Avidyā (nescience), is fully awake. When all beings are said to be awake, i.e., when all beings, who in reality sleep in the night of ignorance, imbued with

the distinct notions of perceiver and things perceived, are as it were dreamers in sleep at night,—that state is night in the eye of the sage who knows the Supreme Reality; for it is nescience itself.

Works are not meant of the Sage.

Wherefore works are enjoined on the ignorant, not on the wise. Wisdom (Vidyā) arising, nescience (Avidyā) disappears as does the darkness of the night at sunrise. Before the dawn of wisdom, nescience presents itself in various forms—as actions, means, and results,—is regarded as authoritative, and becomes the source of all action. When it is regarded as of no authority, it cannot induce action. A man engages in action regarding it as his duty—regarding that action as enjoined by such an authority as the Veda, but not looking upon all this duality as mere illusion, as though it were night. When he has learnt to look upon all this dual world as a mere illusion, as though it were night, when he has realised the Self, his duty consists not in the performance of action, but in the renunciation of all action. Our Lord will accordingly show (v.17 *et seq.*) that such a man's duty consists in devotion to wisdom, in jñāna-nishtha.

(Objection):—In the absence of an injunction (Pravartaka pramāṇa = vidhi) one cannot have recourse to that course either.

(Answer):—This objection does not apply; for the knowledge of Atman means that knowledge of one's own Self. There is indeed no need of an injunction impelling one to devote oneself to one's Atman for the very reason that Atman is one's own very Self. And all organs of knowledge (pramāṇas) are so called because they ultimately lead to a knowledge of the Self. When the knowledge of the true nature of the self has been attained, neither organs of knowledge nor objects of knowledge present themselves to consciousness any longer. For, the final authority, (viz.,

> the Veda), teaches that the Self is in reality no percipient of objects, and while so denying, (i.e., as a result of that teaching), the Veda itself ceases to be an authority in the waking state. In ordinary experience, too, we do not find any organ of knowledge necessitating further operation (on the part of the knower) when once the thing to be perceived by that organ has been perceived.[55]

The following aspects of this commentary command attention. (1) Night is identified with *tamas;* (2) *sleep is identified with avidyā;* (3) *vidyā* removes *avidyā,* as sun removes the darkness of the night; (4) *ātman* is self-evident; and (5) Veda-knowledge is part of the dream (which is part of the night), and this Veda-knowledge also disappears like a dream upon awakening. A good section of the gloss is devoted to Śaṅkara's favorite view that action and knowledge are mutually opposed.

The importance of this passage lies in the fact that it substitutes a two-tier sleep-awake *metaphysical* distinction for the triple stream of consciousness as an *existential* distinction, dreaming being included in sleep, which, here, connotes ignorance per se as opposed to the knowledge of Brahman. The unrealized beings live in ignorance of Brahman and in this state undergo the three states of waking, dreaming, and deep sleep; in fact waking becomes like dreaming, and the distinction between the two can get blurred; and even more so between sleeping and dreaming. That is why Śaṅkara refers to the knowledge of the Veda as *svapnakāla-pramāṇam iva prabodhe.* According to R. C. Zaehner this knowledge of the *jñanī* is twelvefold in content, depending on the understanding of the nature of the 'seeing' in *paśyato*:

> (i) seeing the self (2.29); (ii) seeing the highest (2.59 and n.); (iii) seeing inactivity in action (i.e. the eternal in the temporal) (4.18); (iv) seeing all beings in the self (4.35: 6.29); (v) seeing all beings in God (4.35: 6.30); (vi) seeing that Sāṁkhya and Yoga (theory and practice) are one (5.5); (vii) seeing self in self (6.20: 13.24);

> (viii) seeing self in all beings (6.29); (ix) seeing God everywhere (6.30: 13–27); (x) seeing 'the same' everywhere (6.32: 13. 37–28); (xi) seeing self as not being an agent (13.29: 18.16); (xii) seeing self in transmigration (15.10) and as established in the [empirical] self (15.11).[56]

There are two curious references in *Talks with Sri Ramana Maharshi* that involve reference to both the *Bhagavadgītā* and to sleep. In the first case, Ramaṇa says at one point in his exposition to *Bhagavadgītā* II.12:

> If Self is (nitya) always and (siddha) present, how can there be ajnana? For whom is the ajnana? These are contradictory. But such statements are for guiding the earnest seeker in the right way. He does not readily understand the only Truth if mentioned in plain words as in natwam naham neme janadhipah (not thou, nor I, nor these kings . . .). Sri Krishna declared the Truth, but Arjuna could not grasp it. Later Krishna plainly says that people confound Him with the body, whereas in reality He was not born nor will He die. Still Arjuna requires the whole Gita for the Truth to be made clear to him.
>
> Look, the Self is only Be-ing, not being this or that. It is simple Being. Be—and there is an end of the ignorance. Enquire for whom is the ignorance. *The ego arises when you wake up from sleep. In deep sleep you do not say that you are sleeping and that you are going to wake up or that you have been sleeping so long. But still you are there. Only when you are awake you say that you have slept. Your wakefulness comprises sleep also in it.*[57]

This last sentence seems to restore the inversion of II.69. The second case is provided by the following extract.

> The sleep, dream, samadhi, etc., are all states of the ajnanis. The Self is free from all these. Here is the answer for the former question also.

> D.: I sought to know the state of sthita prajnata (unshaken knowledge).
>
> M.: The sastras are not for the jnani. He has no doubts to be cleared. The riddles are for ajnanis only. The sastras are for them alone.
>
> D.: *Sleep is the state of nescience and so it is said of samadhi also.*
>
> M.: Jnana is beyond knowledge and nescience. There can be no question about that state. It is the Self.[58]

The possibility of the equation of *samādhi* and nescience seems to arise on account of the undifferentiated nature of the two experiences, but they should not be confused no more than being blind and being blindfolded may be confused. Ramaṇa's remark is reminiscent of *Bhagavadgītā* XI.12 that Brahman is neither *sat* not *asat* (but that which illumines both). Moreover, although from an empirical point of view sleep and *samādhi* may afford some parallels, the perspectives diverge radically from a transcendental point of view. In fact Ramaṇa cites from *Bhagavadgītā* II.69 in order to make this point to the lady who

> protested that dream and sleep do not make any appeal to her. She was asked why then she should be careful about her bed unless she courted sleep.
>
> She said that it was for relaxation of the exhausted limbs, rather a state of auto-intoxication. "The sleep state is really dull, whereas the waking state is full of beautiful and interesting things".
>
> M.: What you consider to be filled with beautiful and interesting things is indeed the dull and ignorant state of sleep according to the Jnani:
>
> Ya nisha sarva bhootanam tasyam jagrati samyami.
>
> The wise one is wide awake just where darkness rules for others.
>
> You must certainly wake up from the sleep which is holding you at present.[59]

3

Sleep in *Māṇḍūkyakārikā*

I

One leading Advaitin thinker who preceded Śaṅkara is Gauḍapāda (seventh century), whose *kārikās* or commentarial verses on the *Māṇḍūkya Upaniṣad*[1] have long enjoyed a special status in Advaita.[2] In fact that Upaniṣad itself, despite its brevity, is regarded by many within the Advaitic tradition as containing its quintessence.[3] The basic teaching of the Upaniṣad may be summarized as follows:

> Then the Upaniṣad proceeds to describe the three states of experience. In the state of waking the self consorts with the objects of sense which are external, and its enjoyments are gross. In dreams it revels in a world of images, and its experience is subtle. In sleep there are no desires nor dreams; the self becomes one, without the distinction of seer and seen. It is then a mass of sentience and remains as bliss enjoying bliss. The self of the three states is designated respectively as Vaiśvānara, Taijasa and Prājña. The fourth, Turīya Prājña which is the real self, is beyond the changing modes of existence. It is not caught in the triple stream of waking, dream and sleep, though it is their underlying substrate.

> It is invisible; it is not the content of empirical usage; it cannot be grasped; it does not have identifying marks; it is unthinkable and unnameable; it is the one self which is the essence of consciousness; it is that in which the universe gets resolved; it is tranquil bliss which is non-dual. Thus through a series of negations supplemented by their positive implications, the Māṇḍūkya teaches the real nature of the self.[4]

It is clear that the state of dreamless sleep, designated *prājña*, plays a special role in this scheme, in that it is closest to the state of liberation. But while it is true that as *prājña*, or in the state of dreamless sleep consciousness, the self is devoid of all distinctions, a characteristic of the highest realization, "even here ignorance persists,"[5] while *turīya* or the fourth state is one "untouched by ignorance."[6] *Turīya* is *not* "the massed consciousness of the state of sleep."[7] "It is a state of unalloyed simple consciousness unaffected by experiences. It is therefore *prajñāna ghana*, compacted whole and entire, like sugar candy compacted of sweetness all over."[8]

One may now develop the theme further by comparing the position of the *kārikās*, that is, Gauḍapāda's own position as it emerges through the commentary, with the position of the text, that is to say, the *Māṇḍūkya Upaniṣad* itself. Andrew Fort concludes that "while there are differences of emphasis" in the two texts, "no fundamental philosophical disagreement exists."[9] From the point of view of our study, however, the differences are nevertheless worth noting. Andrew Fort writes:

> Regarding the states, Gauḍapāda basically follows the MāU position. *Turīya* is the non-dual, pervasive substratum of changing consciousness states. Yet he also describes the fourth in more positive (and personal) terminology than does the MāU: it is called ruler, mighty lord (10), and all-seeing (12). It seems to take on the auspicious qualities attributed to the self in the deep sleep in MāU 6, while sleep becomes mere lack of knowledge. Gauḍapāda also more clearly devalues waking and dream.[10]

There are two special features of Gauḍapāda's treatment of deep sleep as such—one physical and the other metaphysical. The physical consists in his assigning an anatomical locus to the *prājña*, or the self in deep sleep. *Prājña* is assigned to the heart, or rather the ether or space of the heart (*hṛdayākāśa*), just as *viśva*, or the self in the waking state, is assigned to the right eye and *taijasa*, or self in the dreaming state, is assigned to the mind. The following description of the self as *prājña* is offered:

> When memory also ceases and sleep supervenes, the self is said to retire into the ether of the heart. The Bṛhadāraṇyaka says, 'When this person full of consciousness is asleep, at that time he absorbs the functions of the organs through his consciousness and lies in the ether which is in the heart'. Here the term 'ether' (*ākāśa*) stands for the supreme self. The meaning is that in sleep one returns to oneself. The assignment of the heart, again, is for the purpose of meditation.[11]

The second special point of Gauḍapāda's treatment of deep sleep consists of the way in which he first spells out its metaphysical dimension and then integrates it with the existential dimension. The metaphysical treatment of deep sleep is already anticipated by the *Bhagavadgītā* and provides both a useful cue and a useful connection here:

> The statement of Gauḍapāda that in the same body, Viśva, Taijasa and Prājña are located is only a prelude to his metaphysical interpretation of the three states, *jāgrat* (waking), *svapna* (dream), and *suṣupti* (sleep). From the metaphysical standpoint the real wakefulness is spiritual awakening (*prabodha*), the so-called state of waking which is empirical is on a par with dream, and sleep is ignorance of the self. What is as night to the ignorant is as day to the wise; and what is as day to the ignorant is as night to the wise. To the knowers of the self the world is non-real; to those who are deluded by nescience the self appears as if non-real.[12]

If we travel down the metaphysical road a little further, we find that what we call ignorance or *avidyā* possesses two properties. It conceals the true nature of a thing, say of a rope as rope or shell as shell. And it then makes it appear as other than what it is—thus the rope is not only *not* perceived as a rope, it is also *mis*perceived as a snake; the shell is not only *not* perceived as a shell, it is *mis*perceived as a piece of silver. Gauḍapāda refers to the first process as *tattvājñāna* (ignorance of the real) and to the second as *anayathā-grahaṇa* (cognizing something other than what it is). Thus the processes of *non-apprehension* and *misapprehension* are connected. This distinction is the key to the rest of his exposition: "The former, according to him, is *nidrā* or sleep (*suṣupti*), and the latter is *svapna* or dream."[12A] Then he integrates this metaphysical understanding with the physiological as follows: in sleep there is only nonapprehension. Hence it corresponds to *ajñāna* (*tattvājñāna*). In waking and dream, however, there is *also anayathāgrahaṇa*, in the form of other positive experiences.

> If we now correlate the three *avasthās* as they are commonly understood and the metaphysical sleep and dream, we shall find that in the state of waking there are both dream and sleep, viz., misapprehension and non-apprehension of the real, in the state of dream there is sleep also, and in the state of sleep there is sleep alone. The metaphysical sleep continues throughout transmigratory life. Its spell is broken only at the onset of knowledge. "When the *jīva* who sleeps on account of the beginningless *māyā* wakes up, he realizes the unborn, sleepless, dreamless, non-dual (*Turīya*)."[13]

In other words, there is metaphysical sleep in all the states, including that of physiological sleep. But these two are *not* identical, because while from physiological sleep one rises on a daily basis, in the case of metaphysical sleep one continues in it on a metempsychotic basis. That is to say: at one level there is only one Sleep from which there is only one Awakening. Within that Sleep is comprised the merry or not so merry-go-round of waking, dreaming, and sleeping. Or to look at it in terms of Sleep: in it there is only dreaming—waking being a form of it—but there is an Awakening possible from it.

II

In the next chapter Śaṅkara's views on sleep will be examined in some detail. He is, after all, the expositor of classical Advaita par excellence. Nevertheless it might be helpful, before one moves toward such a general presentation, to examine his commentary on the *Māṇḍūkyakārikā* on the subject of deep sleep. This will serve to facilitate the transition to the next chapter. Moreover, it will also help broaden the treatment of the subject as a whole, especially if the comparison of his commentary on the *Kārikā* with the *Kārikā* itself enables one to gain further insights into how different Advaitins have approached the phenomenon of deep sleep.

Śaṅkara's treatment of the subject is striking in three respects. At one point Śaṅkara gives a new twist to the threefold classification of the states into waking, dreaming, and sleeping by applying all three to the waking state itself! Andrew Fort notes:

> Śaṅkara's commentary on *kārikā* two takes a surprising turn: he describes the experience (*anubhava*) of the three *pādas* (*viśva*, etc.) *within* the waking state. The *viśva* form is in the right eye and sees what is gross. The *taijasa* form arises in waking when, with eyes closed, one remembers things seen (in the mind) by the eye (we might call this daydreaming or visualization). One now sees forms via internal impressions (*vāsanā*) which consist of light (*tejas*). When even remembering ceases, awareness becomes "massed" (*ekībhūta prājña*) and undifferentiated due to the cessation of mental agitation in waking and dream. Thus the three forms exist in waking: seeing, remembering, and self-absorbed oneness with a "motionless" intellect.[14]

The implications of such a move have not been fully worked out,[15] but if one were to follow through, then sudden enlightenment of the Zen type may become quite consistent with classical Advaita! It will also have the effect, perhaps, of lessening the perception of discontinuity involved in the movement from one state to another.[16] This then would also lessen the sense of discontinuity between sleep and waking.

Although this kind of exposition of the three states within waking is "rare" on the part of Śaṅkara,[17] the fact that it occurs here is not irrelevant in the light of the second striking feature of Śaṅkara's commentary on the *Kārikā*, namely, that herein waking and dreaming tend to be treated on a par by Śaṅkara. Andrew Fort explains:

> Śaṅkara, following Gauḍapāda (in I. 14-6), then says *viśva* (normally waking) and *taijasa* (dreaming) are one class, holding (curiously) dream and sleep in common. This seems to mean that they are subject both to mis- and non-apprehension, as opposed to *prājña*, which does not apprehend reality. It also suggests that the *viśva* and *taijasa* forms of the self are alike in the "dream" of *saṁsāra*, fostering such ideas as "this (child, animal, field) is mine", or "I am happy/sad". *Prājña*, while tied to ignorance and thus causality, has no such delusions. The fourth is sleepless and dreamless, being realized when the delusions of mis- and non-apprehension cease. While Śaṅkara here follows *Gauḍapāda* on the similarity of waking and dreaming in misapprehension of reality, his commentaries, such as the BāU and the *Brahmasūtra-bhāsya*, emphasize that waking is relatively more real than dream.[18]

The fact that in this discussion of the *Kārikā*, waking and dreaming are not yet differentiated as they come to be later, is of a piece with the first striking feature—that Śaṅkara is willing to collapse all the three states within one state.

This leads to the third striking point: that at this stage Śaṅkara distinguishes sharply between all the three empirical states taken together from the transcendental. Thus even when Śaṅkara "finds sleep qualitatively different from the first two states,"[19] it is "still somehow tied to ignorance"[20] and therefore does not mitigate the discontinuity between the empirical states, taken together as a whole, and the transcendental one. However, as Andrew Fort points out, "Śaṅkara gives sleep more exalted status in other, possibly later writings."[21]

This then is the general point to be borne in mind as we move into the next chapter, that the analysis of Śaṅkara's position on sleep, and on the three states in general, could lead one to assign a certain chronological priority to his commentary on the *Kārikā*.

However, the general overall approaches of Gauḍapāda and Śaṅkara do diverge in some respects. This becomes clear, if their approaches are seen in the backdrop of the two older Upaniṣads with an Advaitic orientation—the *Chāndogya* and the *Bṛhadāraṇyaka*. With them in mind:

> One can trace two differing viewpoints among *Advaitins* on the nature of deep sleep. The first claims that in sleep one knows nothing, as if one is "gone to destruction" (ChU, Gauḍapāda). The other (BāU, MāU, Śaṅkara) holds that sleep is a condition of pure bliss and the true form (*svarūpa*) of *brahman*.[22]

It is possible to suggest, in broad terms, that Gauḍapāda's position on sleep is more in line with the *Chāndogya* tradition and that of Śaṅkara more in line with the *Bṛhadāraṇyaka* tradition (as represented by Yājñavalkya). This divergence becomes apparent when their glosses on the *Māṇḍūkya Upaniṣad* are compared:

> Gauḍapāda's *kārikās* show less interest in sleep than in dream and its relation to waking (GK II. 1–15). As in the ChU, deep sleep is ignorance more than blissful unity. The term *suṣupta* is not used in the first *prakaraṇa*; sleep is an aspect of *prājña* (unmodified consciousness, I. 1–4, 11–12). Gauḍapāda emphasizes that sleep is one of the three changing states, different from *turīya*,

the unchanging fourth. He does grant that sleep is not tied to cause and effect (*kārya-kāraṇa*) as are waking and dream; *prājña* is strictly causal.[23]

Moreover,

> In I.13–15, Gauḍapāda refers to *nidrā* (rest, sleep) without dreams, in which one is ignorant of reality. Duality is not perceived (*agrahaṇa*), but lies in seed (*bīja*) form in *nidrā*. In III.34–6, Gauḍapāda also suggests that in sleep the mind (*manas*) passively rests, unlike the properly controlled (*nigṛhīta*) mind. The controlled mind is *brahman*, the ultimate luminous reality beyond dream and sleep.[24]

However, "Śaṅkara does not follow Gauḍapāda's ideas; he aligns himself firmly with the BāU/MāU view. As we saw in his commentary on MāU 5–6, Śaṅkara finds deep sleep to be undifferentiated and blissful consciousness. He also accepts Gauḍapāda's view in I.13–15 that reality is unperceived (*tattva-agrahaṇa*) in sleep,"[25] but for Śaṅkara this is ignorance of a special or specific kind (*viśeṣa*), as revealed by the expressions he employs to designate it—"*upādhi-kṛta-viśeṣa-abhāva* (I.1.9), *viśeṣa-vijñāna-abhāva* (1.3.19), *viśeṣa-vijñāna-upaśama* (III.2.7), and *viśeṣa-saṁjña-abhāva* (IV.4.16)."[26]

We turn now to a consideration of Śaṅkara's general position on deep sleep in more detail.

4

Sleep in Śāṅkara Advaita

I

Śāṅkara Advaita contains several references to the phenomenon of sleep, particularly deep sleep. In this respect one encounters a remarkable statement in his gloss on the *Brahmasūtra* I.4.18, namely, that "It is the general Vedānta doctrine that at the time of deep sleep the soul becomes one with the highest Brahman."[1] This statement might well constitute our point of entrance into the investigation of the role of sleep in Śaṅkara's Advaita. The statement is a powerful one, which also possesses scriptural support. As Śaṅkara remarks in the course of his gloss on *Brahmasūtra* I.3.15:

> For this going of the individual souls into Brahman, which takes place day after day in the state of deep sleep is seen, i.e., is met with in another[2] scriptural passage, viz. Chāndogya Upaniṣad VI.8.1, 'he becomes united with the True'. In ordinary life also we say of a man who lies in deep sleep, 'he has become Brahman', 'he is gone into the state of Brahman.'[3]

However, before long, one finds Śaṅkara equating the state of deep sleep not only with *nirguṇa brahman* but also, in a sense, with *saguṇa brahman*. This is possible because the phenomenon of deep sleep, characterized as it is by the absence of differential consciousness, could be taken to imply either that all such differences have been transcended *or* that they have become latent. In this way it could double for both *nirguṇa* and *saguṇa brahman*. And it does, for he remarks in his gloss on *Brahmasūtra* IV.2.8:

> The *pūrvapakshin* maintains that it is an absolute absorption of the things merged, since it is proved that those things have the highest deity for their causal matter. For it has been established that the deity is the causal substance of all things that have an origin. Hence that passing into the state of non-separation is an absolute one.
>
> To this we reply as follows. Those subtle elements—heat and so on—which constitute the abode of hearing and the other organs persist up to the 'union,' i.e. up to final release from the *saṁsāra*, which is caused by perfect knowledge. 'On account of the declarations of the *saṁsāra* state' made in passage such as 'Some enter the womb, for embodied existence as organic beings; others go into inorganic mater, according to their work and according to their knowledge' (Ka.Up.II, 5, 7). Otherwise the limiting adjuncts of every soul would, at the time of death, be absorbed and the soul would enter into absolute union with Brahman; which would render all scriptural injunction and scriptural doctrine equally purportless. Moreover bondage, which is due to wrong knowledge, cannot be dissolved but through perfect knowledge. Hence, although Brahman is a causal substance of those elements, they are at the time of death—*as in the case of deep sleep and a pralaya of the world—merged in it only in such a way as to continue to exist in a seminal condition.*[4]

Śaṅkara is, however, careful not to equate the state of deep sleep with Īśvara. He writes in his gloss on *Brahmasūtra* I.3.42:

> [His God's] difference from embodied soul in the state of deep sleep is declared in the following passage, 'This person embraced by the intelligent (*prājña*) Self knows nothing that is without, nothing that is within.' Here the term, 'the person,' must mean the embodied soul; for of him it is possible to deny that he knows, because he, as being the knower, may know what is within and without. The 'intelligent Self', on the other hand, is the highest Lord, because he is never dissociated from intelligence, i.e.—in his case—all-embracing knowledge.—Similarly, the passage treating of departure, ie. death ('this bodily Self mounted by the intelligent Self moves along groaning'), refers to the highest Lord as different from the individual Self. There also we have to understand by the 'embodied one' the individual soul which is the Lord of the body, while the 'intelligent one' is again the Lord. We thus understand that 'on account of his being designated as something different, in the states of deep sleep and departure,' the highest Lord forms the subject of the passage.[5]

It is predictably in discussing the state of sleep not in the context of *Brahman*, or Īśvara, but rather the *jīva* that Śaṅkara makes detailed statements that deserve to be cited in extenso. He writes, for instance, in his gloss on *Brahmasūtra* I.1.9:

> With reference to the cause denoted by the word 'Sat,' Scripture says, 'When a man sleeps here, then, my dear, he becomes united with the Sat, he is gone to his own (Self). Therefore they say of him "he sleeps" (svapiti), because he is gone to his own (svam apīta).' (*Ch.* Up. VI.,8, I) This passage explains the well-known verb 'to sleep,' with reference to the soul. The word, 'his own,' denotes the Self which had before been denoted by the word Sat; to the Self he (the individual soul) goes, i.e. into it it is resolved, according to the acknowledged sense of api-i, which means 'to be resolved into.' The individual soul (*jīva*) is called awake as long as being connected with the various external

> objects by means of the modifications of the mind—which thus constitute limiting adjuncts of the soul—it apprehends those external objects, and identifies itself with the gross body, which is one of those external objects. When, modified by the impressions which the external objects have left, it sees dreams, it is denoted by the term 'mind.' When, on the cessation of the two limiting adjuncts (i.e. the subtle and the gross bodies), and the consequent absence of the modifications due to the adjuncts, it is, in the state of deep sleep, merged in the Self as it were, then it is said to be asleep (resolved into the Self). A similar etymology of the word '*hṛdaya*' is given by *śruti*, 'That Self abides in the heart. And this is the etymological explanation: he is in the heart (*hridi ayam*).' (*Ch.* Up. VIII, 3,3.) The words *aśanāya* and *udanyā* are similarly etymologised: 'water is carrying away what has been eaten by him;' 'fire carries away what has been drunk by him' (*Ch.* Up. VI.8,3; 5). Thus the passage quoted above explains the resolution (of the soul) into the Self, denoted by the term '*Sat*,' by means of the etymology of the word 'sleep.' But the intelligent Self can clearly not resolve itself into the non-intelligent *pradhāna*. If, again, it were said that the *pradhāna* is denoted by the word 'own,' because belonging to the Self (as being the Self's own), there would remain the same absurd statement as to an intelligent entity being resolved into a non-intelligent one. Moreover another scriptural passage (viz. 'embraced by the intelligent—*prājña*—Self, he knows nothing that is without, nothing that is within,' *Br.* Up. IV, 3, 21) declares that the soul in the condition of dreamless sleep is resolved into an intelligent entity. Hence that into which all intelligent souls are resolved is an intelligent cause of the world, denoted by the word '*Sat*,' and not the *pradhāna*.—A further reason for the pradhāna not being the cause is subjoined.[6]

The metaphor of sleep is subsequently extended to that of "universal sleep":

> A previous stage of world such as the one assumed by us must necessarily be admitted, since it is according to sense and reason. For without it the highest Lord could not be conceived as creator, as he could not become active if he were destitute of the potentiality of action. The existence of such a causes potentiality renders it moreover possible that the released should not enter on new courses of existence, as it is destroyed by perfect knowledge. For that causal potentiality is of the nature of Nescience; it is rightly denoted by the term 'undeveloped;' it has the highest Lord for its substratum; it is of the nature of an illusion; it is a universal sleep in which are lying the transmigrating souls destitute for the time of the consciousness of their individual character.[7]

The fact that in sleep distinctions disappear only to reappear, that they are experientially suspended rather than ontologically eliminated, enables Śaṅkara to answer his opponent as follows in his gloss on *Brahmasūtra* II.1.9:

> With regard to the second objection, viz. that if we assume all distinctions to pass (at the time of reabsorption) into the state of non-distinction there would be no special reason for the origin of a new world affected with distinctions, we likewise refer to the 'existence of parallel instances.' For the case is parallel to that of deep sleep and trance. In those states also the soul enters into an essential condition of non-distinction; nevertheless, wrong knowledge being not yet finally overcome, the old state of distinction re-establishes itself as soon as the soul awakes from its sleep or trance, compare the scriptural passage, 'All these creatures when they have become merged in the True, know not that they are merged in the True. Whatever these creatures are here, whether a lion, of a wolf, or a boar, or a worm, or a midge, or a gnat, or a musquito, that they become again' (*Ch.* Up. VI, 9, 2; 3). For just as during the subsistence of the world the phenomenon of multifarious

> distinct existence, based on wrong knowledge, proceeds unimpeded like the vision of a dream, although there is only one highest Self devoid of all distinction; so, we conclude, there remains, even after reabsorption, the power of distinction (potential distinction) founded on wrong knowledge.—Herewith the objection that—according to our doctrine—even the finally released souls would be born again is already disposed of. They will not be born again because in their case knowledge has been entirely discarded by perfect knowledge.[8]

To turn back to the *jīva* itself, Śaṅkara tries to associate sleep with the psychophysical dimension of the living being as adumbrated in Vedānta. In his gloss on *Brahmasūtra* III.2.7 he discusses the scriptural passages that associate deep sleep with the *nāḍīs* (or nerves) and remarks:

> Although in another text the *nāḍīs* are spoken of as an independent place of deep sleep as it were ('then he has entered into those *nāḍīs*'), yet, in order not to contradict other passages in which Brahman is spoken of as the place of deep sleep, we must explain that text to mean that the soul abides in Brahman through the *nāḍīs*. Nor is this interpretation opposed to the employment of the locative case ('into—or in—those *nāḍīs*'); for if the soul enters into Brahman by means of the *nāḍīs* it is at the same time in the *nāḍīs*; just as a man who descends to the sea by means of the river Gaṅgā is at the same time on the Gaṅgā.[9]

He then tackles the passages which locate deep sleep within the pericardium.

> Analogously we conclude that the pericardium also, because it is mentioned in a passage treating of Brahman, is a place of deep sleep only in subordination to Brahman. For the ether within the heart is at first spoken of as the place of sleep ('He lies in the ether

> which is in the heart,' *Br.* Up. II, I, 17), and with reference thereto it is said later on, 'He rests in the pericardium' (II, I, 19). Pericardium (*purītat*) is a name of that which envelops the heart; hence that which rests within the ether of the heart—which is contained in the pericardium—can itself be said to rest within the pericardium; just as a man living in a town surrounded by walls is said to live within the walls. That the ether within the heart is Brahman has already been shown (I, 3, 14).—That again the *nāḍīs* and the pericardium have to be combined as places of deep sleep appears from their being mentioned together in one sentence ('Through them he moves forth and rests in *purītat*). That that which is (*sat*) and the intelligent Self (*prājña*) are only names of Brahman is well known; hence scripture mentions only three places of deep sleep, viz. the *nāḍīs*, the pericardium, and Brahman.[10]

An important question in Śaṅkara's description of sleep is related to its association with bliss. He remarks on this connection in the gloss on *Brahmasūtra* I.3.8:

> The word 'bliss' (saṁprasāda) means that state of deep sleep, as may be concluded, firstly, from the etymology of the word ('In it he, i.e. man, is altogether pleased—saṁprasīdati')—and, secondly, from the fact of saṁprasāda being mentioned in the Bṛhadāraṇyaka together with the state of dream and the waking state.[11]

He also cites *Praśna Upaniṣad* IV.6 in support of this association.[12]

Clearly, however, the bliss of deep sleep is not identical with that of *Brahman*. Śaṅkara even distinguishes between the bliss of the *ānandamaya kośa* and the bliss of *Brahman* in the *Chāndogya*. Therefore he clarifies his reference to the passage in the *Praśna Upaniṣad* in his gloss on *Brahmasūtra* I.3.9 as follows: "The bliss also of which the [said] Scripture speaks as connected with that state [of bliss] is mentioned only in order to show that bliss constitutes the nature of the self."[13]

This brief survey of Śaṅkara's views must now make way for a more critical focus on the main issues involved.

II

The claim that a state of unconsciousness holds the key to the mystery of consciousness constitutes a paradox. One may begin by reviewing Śaṅkara's attempts at resolving this paradox.

Śaṅkara's resolution can be broken down in to three stages. First of all, he establishes that consciousness persists in deep sleep, even if we are not conscious of it. This is established on empirical grounds. Why we are unconscious of it, though consciousness is present, is established next. This is done on logical grounds. Finally, the question may be asked: does the explanation that one is conscious, though apparently unconscious during sleep, also apply to states of unconsciousness other than sleep, such as fainting, etc.? This question is answered on conceptual grounds.

How can one maintain that one is conscious in deep sleep in any sense, when in dreamless sleep "one becomes here oblivious of the world and even of his own existence."[14] The answer

> occurs in the second chapter of the prose section of the *Upadeśasāhasrī*. After reviewing the reasons for Advaita's view on the nonact (*sic*) and the persisting nature of consciousness, an important objection is raised by the pupil in the dialogue. In deep sleep consciousness ceases; we say, 'I knew nothing.' And thus consciousness is adventitious after all. The teacher replies that the pupil's analysis of deep sleep is incorrect. How could we know enough to report that we knew nothing in deep sleep unless we were conscious during that period? It is that consciousness, which is never lost, that is constitutive of the true Self about which the pupil asks.[15]

The logical explanation of this unconscious consciousness in dreamless sleep is offered by Śaṅkara "by claiming that the absence of knowledge in deep sleep is a consequence of the absence of anything experienced separate from consciousness, rather than the absence of consciousness itself."[16]

The third stage is more difficult to handle. How is the unconsciousness in dreamless sleep to be differentiated, if at all from coma, fainting, etc.? William Indich recognizes at the very start that this is a difficult philosophical problem in general, not just for Śaṅkara, and remarks: "Clearly, the problem presented to Śaṅkara in this context involves the question of just what a phenomenal or life experience is, and just what point life experience itself ends and death begins. In fact, this is a question with respect of which physicians, lawyers and ethicists are still very much in conflict today."[17] He also observes that "Śaṅkara concludes his discussion by conceding that we ought to grant these states status of their own, although they are relatively rare and by implication, perhaps, are not very central to his theory of consciousness."[18]

I have cited these remarks to indicate that Indich is not unsympathetic to Śaṅkara in general, but even he is forced to ask: "Where is the beef?" He writes:

> Śaṅkara's not altogether satisfactory answer to this question consists in maintaining that there is partial agreement between these various unconscious conditions and both deep sleep and death. These conditions are both superficially similar to sleep, in the sense that both represent an absence of waking and dream consciousness, and to death, in the sense that people frequently pass away after having been in these states for some time. On the other hand, Śaṅkara has to confess that there is not much real similarity between these conditions and either sleep or death, since the causes, physiological and phenomenological characteristics, etc., which distinguish unconsciousness from both sleep and death are quite great.[19]

Indich also wonders why Śaṅkara did not use all the intellectual resources available to him in Advaita for coming to grips with the issue, perhaps satisfactorily.

Each of the three arguments extracted from Śaṅkara now need to be presented in more historical and phenomenological detail to be fully appreciated and assessed.

The basic evidence adduced to establish that sleep is not identical with unconsciousness is that there persists the consciousness of having been unconscious, or the knowledge that one did not know. This argument is not new to Advaita. It is also used in Yoga, when sleep is discussed as a modification of the mind or *citta-vṛtti*:

> Sleep (nidrā) is another kind of mental modification (citta-vṛtti). It is due to the preponderance of tamas in citta and the consequent cessation of waking consciousness and dream experiences. If thus stands for deep dreamless sleep (suṣupti). Some philosophers think that in sound sleep there is no mental function or conscious state at all. But this is wrong. On waking from sound sleep we say, 'I slept well', 'I knew nothing', etc. Such memory of what took place during sleep supposes direct experience of the state of sleep. So there must be in sleep some cognitive mental state or process which is concerned in the experience of the absence of knowledge (abhāvapratyayālambanā vṛtti).[20]

The same point may be presented in more phenomenological terms as follows:

> The Advaitin argues that in the state of deep sleep, consciousness is present, that deep sleep is a state of consciousness and not of non-consciousness, although there are no objects there with which it relates or interacts. And this is because upon returning to waking consciousness, one does affirm that 'I had a wonderful sleep'. If consciousness were absent altogether in that state, no memory affirmation of it would be possible. Consciousness, it is believed, thus persists even in the absence of all of the instruments of sense and cognitive experience.[21]

The strict Advaitin argument—though it arrives at the same conclusion—has to arrive at it differently, because according to Advaita the mind or *antaḥkaraṇa* ceases to function, unlike in Yoga, in deep sleep. *It is not because of the presence of the mind but because of the presence of sākṣī that the persistence of identity is established.*

> Awake by day, going to sleep by night and experiencing a dream in the midst of his sleep the same person exclaims: I am awake now, I slept last night and I had a dream. This sense of I is continuous with all these three states, even though as was pointed out earlier, *jāgrat, svapna* and *suṣupti* are exclusive of one another. By what is this personal identity established in the three states referring them all to the same individual? Thus 'I' common to the three states bears witness to waking-like experiences, to the dream events and by virtue of the *pratyabhijñā* referred to earlier,[22] to the persistence of consciousness in dreamless sleep. This awareness which underlies them all is said to be 'the witnessing consciousness' or as it is called *sākṣicaitanya*.[23]

The fact that there is the existence of consciousness in some form in sleep per se, not *merely* its persistence, has to do with the Advaitin doctrine of the self-luminosity of consciousness—or that it can be a pure subject without an object, keeping in mind Citsukha's definition of it as "the capacity of being called immediately known in empirical usage while not being an object of cognition."[24] It would now be clear why

> deep sleep plays an important part in the debate concerning the self-luminosity of consciousness. The Advaitin is committed to the doctrine of the essential luminosity of the Self as well as the claim that nothing is perceived or known in the sleep state. His opponents object, however, that these two positions are contradictory since a state in which nothing is perceived or known is actually an unconscious state, i.e.,

> a state in which luminous consciousness is absent. Śaṅkara argues that the blissful nature of sleep experience can only be explained as a presentation of self-luminous consciousness to itself, since all other modes of awareness are in their latent condition.[25]

It must not be overlooked that although luminosity is *present* in deep sleep, it is also in *eclipse*. The situation may be summarized as follows:

> the *ātman* is *sat, cit* and *ānanda*. During sleep when it is shrouded by *māyā*, its *cit* aspect suffers an eclipse. It remains, however, behind the cloud of *māyā;* as *cit*. It is not as if the *ātman* is not. It is as *sanmātram* in the language of the *śloka*. Also the *ānanda* aspect of the *ātman* too is present. For, on waking, the man says: I slept happily (*sukham asvāpsam*). The *sukha* is the *ānanda* of the *ātman*. Only, it is neither superabundant nor superexcellent as the *ānanda* of Brahmānubhava in the super-conscious state of transcendentally wakeful experience of identity with Brahman.[26]

It can also be elaborated with the help of the sixth verse of *Śrī Dakṣiṇāmūrtistotra* ascribed to Śaṅkara,[27] as follows:

> There is distinct cognition of gross and subtle objects respectively in *jāgrat* and in *svapna*. But during sleep, when the dream is over, there is no sense-organ activity, and there is a stillness of the mind, *manolaya*. So there is no discriminative awareness of objects. There is no *viseśajñāna* because the sense-organs have subsided into their activating causes. Is the *cit* which is the *ātman* present then? Does it shine? Yes; says the *śloka*. It does in the same way as the sun and moon do during a eclipse, not brightly however, but hidden by the eclipsing agent. Though sun and moon are invisible during the eclipse, we infer their continued existence abiding before, during and after the eclipse. We

> say that during the eclipse the sun was the same that it was before and that it shines after it is over. Even so, in the case of the man who sleeps, his *cit* is shrouded by *māyā*. When he wakes from his sleep, he establishes in his consciousness a continuity of his personal identity before, during, and after sleep. This gives expression to when, on waking from his sleep, he says: I slept happily; I did not know anything. The awareness of self-identity is called *pratyabhijñā*. To Śrī Daksiṇāmūrti who is the Supreme Self with whom this *pratyabhijñā* is associated, I make this salutation.[28]

The question regarding states of unconsciousness that are similar to deep sleep but not identical with it remains to be tackled. The swoon would be an example of such a state. The following extended extract from Śaṅkara's commentary on *Brahmasūtra* III.2.10 is required to carry the discussion further.

> *Opponent*: Let it be then that he is in deep sleep, since he has no consciousness at the same time that he is not dead.
>
> *Vedāntin*: Not so, for there is a difference. A man in a swoon may not breathe for a long time, but his body may be in tremors and his face may be distorted (with a look of terror), and the eyes may remain wide open. But a man in deep sleep has a calm face, he breathes rhythmically again and again, his eyes remain closed, and his body has no contortion. A sleeping man is awakened simply by pushing him with the hand, whereas an unconscious man cannot be brought back to consciousness even by beating with a club. Furthermore, the causes of swoon and sleep differ, for fainting results from blows from a club etc., while sleep comes as a result of fatigue. And people never acknowledge that a man under a swoon sleeps. By a process of elimination we realize that swooning away is a state of half sleep; for he is not fully asleep as his state is different for sleep.

> *Opponent*: How again can a swoon be described as a partial sleep. Since with regard to the sleeping man the Upaniṣads say, "O amiable one, he then becomes unified with Existence" (Ch. VI.viii.1), "In this state a thief is no thief" (Br. IV.iii.22), "Night and day do not overflow this embankment (i.e. Brahman), nor old age, nor death, nor sorrow, nor merit, nor demerit" (Ch. VIII.iv.1)? For an individual being gets the results of merit and demerit through the generation of the ideas of his being happy or sorry; but neither the idea of happiness nor of misery exists in sleep; so also they are absent in a swoon. Hence it follows that in a swoon, as in sleep, there is a complete merger in Existence owing to the cessation of the limiting adjuncts; but it is not a partial merger.
>
> *Vedāntin*: With regard to this the answer is, that it is not our view that in a swoon a man becomes half merged in Brahman.
>
> *Opponent*: What do you say then?
>
> *Vedāntin*: A swoon is partially a form of sleep, and partially of some other state. We have already shown its similarity and dissimilarity with sleep. And it is a door to death. So long as the individual's *karma* lasts, his speech and mind return from a swoon; but when the *karma* has no residue, his breathing and warmth depart. Hence the knowers of Brahman call swoon a partial sleep. As for the objection raised that no fifth state is known to exist, that is nothing damaging. On account of being a casual state, it is not so widely known; and yet it is well recognized in this world and in the books of medicine. By admitting it to be a partial sleep, we do not reckon it to be a fifth state. In this way it is all beyond criticism.[29]

The point to be noted here is that Śaṅkara's main term of reference is an analysis of three *natural* states of consciousness, and swoon, coma, etc. are clearly abnormal states. In other words, Śaṅkara's discussion of deep sleep is essentially a discussion of normal deep sleep and the unconsciousness associated with such normal deep sleep. Such unconsciousness has two conditions associated with it: (1) the experience of deep sleep unconsciousness is beyond the pale of *karma*[30] and (2) is therefore characterized by a taste of Ātmic bliss and *not* karmic joys or sorrows.[31]

The tenor of Śaṅkara's discussion suggests that this is *not* the case with swoon or coma. They may even be treated as karmic consequences undergone in the waking state involving elements of unconsciousness, etc. In this context William Indich also makes the following remark:

> Note that Śaṅkara fails to treat death as a level of conscious experience. One wonders why Śaṅkara does not try to use even death to support his argument for the persistence of consciousness by drawing, for example, upon traditional statements indicating that death itself is followed by consciousness, either in terms of rebirth into the phenomenal world or in terms of liberation.[32]

It seems to me, on closer inspection, that perhaps Śaṅkara's failure to exploit these possibilities has some reasons underlying them. In order to establish the cogency of these reasons, let us first consider an account of the process of dying from a late Advaita text, the *Advaita Bodha Dīpikā*.

> D.: How can Birth and Death be illusory?
>
> M.: Listen carefully to what I say.
>
> 107–109. Just as when *jīva* is overcome by sleep, the bearings of the waking state give place to new ones of dream in order to reproduce past experiences, or there is total loss of all external things and mental activities, so also when he is overpowered by coma before death the present bearings are lost and the mind lies dormant. *This is death.* When the mind resumes the reproduction of past experiences in new settings, the phenomenon is *called birth*. The process of birth starts with the man's imagining "Here is my mother; I lie in her womb; my body has those limbs". Then he

> imagines himself born into the world, and later says "This is my father; I am his son; my age is such and such; these are my relatives and friends; this fine house is mine" and so on. This series of new illusions begins with the loss of former illusions in the coma before death, and depends upon the results of past actions.
>
> 110–113. The *jīva* overpowered by the unreal coma before death has different illusions according to his different past actions. After death, he believes "Here is heaven; it is very lovely; I am in it; I am now a wonderful celestial being; so many charming celestial damsels are at my service; I have nectar for drink", or, "Here is the region of Death; here is the God of Death; these are the messengers of Death; oh! They are so cruel—they pitch me into hell!" or, "Here is the region of the *pitṛs*; or of Brahmā; or of Viṣṇu; or of Śiva" and so on. Thus according to their nature, the latencies of past *karma* present themselves before the Self, who remains always the unchanging Ether of Consciousness, as illusions of birth, death, passage to heaven, hell or other regions. They are only delusions of the mind and not real.[33]

If Śaṅkara held such a view of the process of death and rebirth, then William Indich's remarks would seem justified. But this does not seem to have been the case, as is obvious from the following reconstruction by Karl H. Potter.

> The Upaniṣads offer several accounts of what happens to these various things at the time of death. It is not altogether easy to rationalize all these into a consistent account. What I provide is a reconstruction which follows Śaṅkara where there are disagreements. The process goes as follows:
>
> (i). The speech-function becomes absorbed into the intellectual organ, or power of thought (*manas*). The dying man stops speaking.

(ii) It is followed by the functions of all the other organs. Śaṅkara emphasizes that it is only the functions which merge, not the organs themselves. One must keep in mind that a sense-organ, for example, is not to be confused with its physical locus—the visual organ is different from the eyeball.

(iii) Then the *manas*, having absorbed these various functions, has its own functions absorbed into breath (*prāṇa*). *That this is so is evidenced by the fact that dying persons—and for that matter those asleep and not dreaming—are seen to breathe although their senses and mind are not functioning.*

(iv) Next, breath so endowed merges with the individual self (*jīva*), that is, with the internal organ as limited by the awarenesses, karmic residues, and *vāsanās* present at this moment. The man stops breathing.

(v) Now the *jīva*, thus encumbered, joins the subtle elements (*tanmātra*). These are five in number, corresponding to the five gross elements—air, fire, earth, water, and *ākāśa*. These "subtle" elements are apparently conceived of as minute particles which form the seeds from which their gross counterparts grow. The cluster of the five subtle elements provides a (material) "subtle body" (*sūkṣmaśarīra*) which now encloses the *jīva* with its appurtenances, just as the gross body did during life.

(vi) All these factors collect in the "heart". The *jīva* arrives replete with awareness (both true and false), karmic residues, *vāsanās*, desires, and internal organs, *so it is perfectly capable of consciousness. However, since the external organs have stopped functioning, its consciousness at this point, like consciousness in dreams, is completely controlled by past karma.* Thus at this "moment of death" the *jīva* is caused by its karma to develop a *vāsanā* which determines the direction in which the subtle body will go as it leaves the "heart"—by which veins and point of egress, by what path, and to what kind of birth it will eventually proceed.

(vii) Thus decided, the *jīva*-controlled subtle body leaves the "heart" by one or another of the many veins and arteries, eventually gaining egress from the dead gross body by one or another aperture.

> To this point, the Upanisadic sources appear relatively consistent in their implications. When they turn to the account of what happens immediately after death the versions diverge slightly.[34]

It is clear that although unconsciousness as an element in the dying process is indeed mentioned, it is the element of consciousness in the process that is far more significant. The same holds for the *jīva* en route to its new incarnation.

> How does the passage along these paths take place? In the Bṛhadāraṇyaka Upaniṣad we are told that the self proceeds from this body to the next like a leech or a caterpillar; Śaṅkara comments that the idea is that the self creates a link from the old body to the new by means of its vasanas. *This serves to remind us that as the self encased in its subtle body moves along its path it is not unconscious*—it is having experiences, determined by its karmic residues, as in a dream, and is forming plans and following them out as it goes along. It is thus exhausting some of its stored-up karmic residues as it proceeds, and continues doing so in the "heaven" or "hell" (sun, moon, or Samyamana) at which it in due course arrives.[35]

It is clear now why Śaṅkara could not use the idea that "death itself is followed by consciousness," because within the framework he was working, it is *itself* characterized by consciousness.

It may be possible to tie these themes together in the following way. One can distinguish, I think, from an Advaitic point of view, between three *saṁsāras*. First of all there is the *daily saṁsāra* of the three states of consciousness—waking, dreaming, and deep sleep, which we experience every day. Then there is the *reincarnatory saṁsāra*, in which one moves on from one life to another. The third *saṁsāra* is a misnomer—it is no *saṁsāra* at all. It is the *saṁsāra beyond saṁsāra*—namely, Liberation.

It seems that the parameters of Śaṅkara's discussion of deep sleep are really provided by the first kind of *saṁsāra*. His basic position may first be identified by the way he opens his commentary on the *Brahmasūtra*,

> with the statement of the existence of the pure Self free from any impurity as the ultimate truth. This is affirmed on the authority of the Upaniṣads. Our experience is based on an identification of the Self with the body, the senses, etc. This is the beginningless *māyā*. In our waking life we identify the Self with many unreal things but in dreamless sleep, when we are free from phenomenal notions, the nature of our true state as blessedness is partially realised.[36]

Śaṅkara argues that the Self is of the "nature of pure consciousness and it is permanent and not momentary,"[37] and that the state of blessedness is only *partially* realized, in deep sleep. Why?

It is now time to introduce the concept of nescience or *avidyā* in the context of this discussion. In standard Advaita, which Śaṅkara was so instrumental in formulating, the doctrine of nescience and deep sleep are closely connected. This connection has been lucidly explained by M. Hiriyanna.[38] Here we face a somewhat different issue, namely, whether according to Śaṅkara deep sleep is characterized by nescience or not.

The problem arises because Śaṅkara makes two apparently contradictory statements on this point. In his gloss on

Bṛhadāraṇyaka Upaniṣad he states that there is no *avidyā* in sleep, while in his gloss on *Chāndogya Upaniṣad* he states the contrary—that *avidyā* exists in sleep.[39] T. M. P. Mahadevan has drawn attention to this conflict and also to how Sarvajñātman (tenth century) tries to resolve it.

> Sarvajñātman solves this problem by interpreting the statement, that avidyā does not exist in sleep, as meaning that avidyā is not determinately perceived in sleep in the form 'I am ignorant'. This is how he explains the presence of ignorance in sleep, although it is not experienced then. When a person wakes up from sleep he infers that the entire universe was merged in avidyā in the state of sleep in its subtle form. This is not known in the state of deep sleep, because the merging is not experienced at that time. Addressing a disciple, Sarvajñātman says: "Your avidyā alone is experienced then in deep-sleep for on waking up you say 'I did not know anything when I was asleep'. If avidyā is not known in deep sleep through experience then how could there be the later reminiscence in the form 'I did not know anything'. So be certain on the authority of experience that avidyā exists and is experienced in deep-sleep". As the state of deep-sleep is devoid of the function of intellect, avidyā is not determinately perceived them. But having given rise to intellect in the waking state, avidyā becomes the object of experience such as 'I do not know' and 'I am ignorant'.[40]

The issue arises, that if *avidyā* is not conceded in the state of deep sleep, then how is that state to be distinguished from Realization? Even as it is, the two states are considered so close that they could be conflated. For instance, when the waking state is called *viśva*, and the dreaming *taijasa*, then the state of deep sleep is called *prājña*. *Māṇḍūkya Upaniṣad* V reads:

> 5. Where one, being fast asleep, does not desire any desire whatsoever and does not see any dream whatsoever, that is deep sleep. The third quarter is prājña,

> whose sphere (of activity) is the state of deep sleep, who has become one, who is verily, a mass of cognition, who is full of bliss and who enjoys (experiences) bliss, whose face is thought.[41]

The description is very similar to the state of liberation. The *Chāndogya Upaniṣad* (VIII.3.2) declares, as noted earlier, "Just as those who do not know the field walk again and again over the hidden treasure of gold and do not find it, even so all creatures here go day after day into the Brahma-world and yet do not find it, for they are carried away by untruth."[42] Śaṅkara clearly states that the reference here is to deep sleep (*suṣuptikāla*).[43]

Modern writers on Śaṅkara have asserted that according to Śaṅkara "the absence of duality in sleep reveals the non-dual nature of absolute consciousness itself";[44] and modern Advaitins like Ramaṇa clearly treat the experience of deep sleep as paradigmatic of, if not actually of, Realization, when they claim that "deep sleep is nothing but the experience of pure *being*."[45] The *Tripurā Rahasya* is equally forthright in its statements:

> The concentration is possible that in deep sleep and samadhi, the Self remains unqualified and therefore is not identical with the limited consciousness of the ego, 'I' in the wakeful state. The answer is as follows: 'I', is of two kinds—qualified and unqualified. Qualification implies limitations whereas its absence implies its unlimited nature.
>
> 'I' is associated with limitations in dream and wakeful states, and it is free from them in deep slumber and Samadhi states.
>
> In that case is the 'I' in Samadhi or sleep associated with trifold division of subject, object, and their relation? No! Being pure and single, it is unblemished and persists as 'I-I', and nothing else. The same is Perfection.[46]

The case becomes even more serious when the opponent claims that "you certainly cannot admit any connection of the soul with the intellect during sleep." To this, *Brahmasūtra* II.3.31 furnishes a reply. As Śaṅkara explains:

> We see in the world that manhood etc. though existing all the time in a latent state, are not perceived during boyhood etc. and are thus treated as though non-existent, but they become manifest in youth etc.; and it is not a fact that they evolve out of nothing, for in that case even a eunuch should grow those (moustaches etc.). Similarly, too, the contact with the intellect etc. remains in a state of latency during sleep and dissolution, and emerges again during waking and creation. For thus alone it becomes logical. Nothing can possibly be born capriciously, for that would lead to unwarranted possibilities (of effects being produced without causes). The Upaniṣad also shows that this waking from sleep is possible because of the existence of ignorance in a seed form (remaining dormant in sleep): "Though unified with Existence (Brahman) in sleep, they do not understand, 'We have merged in Existence'. They return here as a tiger or a lion" (just as they had been here before) (Ch. VI.ix.3.) etc. Hence it is proved that the contact with the intellect etc. persists as long as the individuality of the soul lasts.[47]

The point to note here is that *latent* contact with the intellect persists, for *antaḥkaraṇa* is withdrawn in *avidyā* with which the Self is in contact, in deep sleep. But according to Śaṅkara, *avidyā* (or *māyā*) is one, *not many*.[48] And this generates a major question: how does the *jīva* survive this dissolution of individuality into a mass of undifferentiatedness, to emerge from it with the sense of individuality, which was temporarily lost, intact.

This problem has another side to it: even in Brahman-realization the sense of individuality is lost, so how does one emerge from that with a sense of individuality intact? In other words, at the highest point of unification of consciousness the issue is the same—whether *vidyā* or *avidyā* is involved. No doubt the contents differ—it is *vidyā* in one case and *avidyā* in another—yet the structure of the problem is the same. Whether I have dissolved in light or in darkness, how do I regain my original configuration, having lost it?

A metaphor that appears in Śaṅkara's gloss on *Brahmasūtra* III.2.9 is illuminating on this point. The "opponent" says:

> When a drop of water is thrown into a mass of water, it becomes one with that mass. And when an attempt is made to take it up again from there, it is impossible to have that very same drop. Similarly when the sleeping soul has become one with the supreme Self and has attained quiescence (i.e. freedom from everything), that very soul cannot wake up again. Hence the conclusion is that the waking being may be either the original soul, or he may be God, or some other individual soul.[49]

After answering the opponent on the basis of "reasons of action, remembrance, scriptural authority and injunction,"[50] Śaṅkara addresses the metaphor:

> And it was argued that just as a drop of water thrown into a mass of water cannot be singled out, so also a soul merging in Existence cannot spring up again. That is being refuted. In the analogy it is quite in order to say that the (selfsame) drop of water cannot be singled out, since there is nothing to mark out its individuality. But here we have karma and ignorance as the factors making the (individual) distinction. The two cases are thus different.[51]

One can perhaps refine the position further. When the Realized one regains his individuality after *samādhi*, it is due to (past) karma or *prārabdha* alone. When the ignorant one rises from sleep, such a one regains individuality on account of *both* continuing *avidyā* and *karma*.

This then raises the question: what quality does the dreamless sleep of the Jñānī possess? One way of answering this question would be to say that the Jñānī knows *avidyā* to be *vidyā* in the same way as what may be first considered darkness as something opposed to light, comes to be regarded as a shadow or shade complementary to light.

It may require an effort of imagination to visualize certain possibilities: that a single entity may generate its own counterpart. If it be suggested that light creates darkness or shadow, then the need for an obstructing medium may be pointed out, although sunspots are known to occur on the sun. Fire generating smoke, which may conceal it, would be another example, but that too is not without its problems.

But consider the following. In the solar system originally there was only the sun. From that sun the earth emerged and cooled down sufficiently, at least on the surface, for life to emerge. Then human beings appeared with an ability to wonder at nature—and above all the sun. That very sun acting on the water that appeared on the earth, which it itself brought into being, generates clouds. And these clouds, its own secondary creation, block the vision of its own sentient creation, the human beings, as they wish to look at the sun! Moreover, they can only look at it in its own light. Is there anything then which, howsoever different from the sun, cannot be brought in relation to the sun?[52]

5

Sleep in Later Advaita

It has been said that "most later *Advaitins* largely accepted Śaṅkara's views on dream and deep sleep, finding all states illusory, dream even less real than waking, and an ambiguity between sleep as ignorance and/or bliss. The only immediate disciple of Śaṅkara who writes at any length on dream and sleep is Sureśvara."[1] We turn now to an examination of his views on sleep. In his well-known work *Naiṣkarmyasiddhi* (IV.42.3) he "merely quotes Gauḍapāda's *Kārikās* (I.15) and Śaṅkara's *Upadeśasāhasrī* (17.26), holding that waking and dream falsely apprehend duality and that sleep is ignorant of reality and the *tāmasic* seed of waking and dream."[2] His *Bṛhadāraṇyakopaniṣad-vārttika*, on the other hand, provides "illuminating references to sleep."[3]

Sureśvara's treatment of sleep contains some interesting features, one of which is the attention he attaches to dreaming so as to virtually subsume it under waking. As a result the contrast of both waking *and* dreaming with sleep is heightened:

> Waking is mentioned generally only in relation to dreaming. Sureśvara's main point about waking is its bondage to action (*karma*) via its 'helpers': body, senses, and the sun. Waking's helpers are generally contrasted

with dream's 'mere' mental images (*vāsanā* and *bhāvanā* are used interchangeably here) or sleep's detached, serene rest.[4]

Moreover,

> Sureśvara, following Śaṅkara, argues that the apparent dream world is unreal; the self illumines *vāsanās* via the intellect (*buddhi, antaḥkaraṇa*) alone, without the help of sun or eye. Further, there is no basis for, or means of, motion in dream (the body is seen motionless), there is no room in the body for dream sights, and no results of actions are seen by others. Dream experience also arises from waking action, as a dreamed king and his activity derive from, and are not the same as, a 'real' (existent in waking) king.[5]

Furthermore, the contrasting of waking and dreaming has the result of ontologically undermining both:

> Dreaming and waking are alike, however, in being transient and conditioned. What is 'real' in one state is illusion (*mṛṣā*) in the other; Sureśvara uses the example of a person hungry in waking, but full in dream, and vice versa. According to Sureśvara, the states (specially waking and dream) alternate back and forth, and apparently co-create each other. *Vāsanās* cause desires and actions upon waking, which then cause *vāsanās* in dream. There is an endlessly reinforcing cycle of dream *vāsanās* acquired from waking action again creating waking actions.[6]

This produces some curious results. The body comes off better than the mind in a sense, as "while sleeping, *the body is pervaded by equanimous consciousness* in all directions and one goes to the highest end."[7] His overall position on deep sleep also raises interesting issues.

> For Sureśvara, deep sleep (often called *saṁprasāda* or *prājña*) is unconditioned luminousness, clearly a precursor to experiencing the bliss of *brahman*. The self in

> sleep is separated from the body with its ignorance, desire, and action. Sleep has no "lower" seeing or particularized knowledge (*viśeṣa-jñāna*) as in waking and dream, just pure consciousness pervasively illumining like the sun.
>
> Sleep is the causal seed of other states, which shows its primacy, but also its connection with ignorance and dullness. There is an interesting ambiguity in Sureśvara's description of sleep's ignorance. Sometimes he says sleep contains ignorance, at other times he says there is no ignorance in sleep. By "no ignorance," he seems to mean "no awareness" of a specific thing. The exact nature of ignorance (in sleep and through all states) could have been made clearer here, and is much discussed in later *Advaita*.[8]

In all this he maintains the central thrust of Advaita. But he is also significant for indicating two lines of Advaitic doctrinal developments around sleep that later get marginalized. One of them pertains to the application of the trichotomy of the three states of waking, dreaming, and sleeping within one state, such as that of waking, as attempted by Śaṅkara.[9] Sureśvara carries this process forward in his *Bṛhadāraṇyaka-Upaniṣad-Bhāṣya Vārtikka* (IV.3.1055–59).

> . . . Sureśvara in one place subdivides each state into three. This shows an awareness of the complexity within a "single" state and a desire to clarify further the nature of ever-fluctuating states. Waking-waking is rational awareness, waking-dream is erroneous perception, waking-sleep is not-attachment to objects, dream-waking is acting as if awake in dream, dream-dream is dream within a dream, dream-sleep is a forgotten dream, sleep-waking is foolishness, sleep-dream is peacefulness, sleep-sleep is ingorance of the one reality. The self witnesses all the states, of course.[10]

This trend fades away subsequently in Advaita, although some traces of it survive in modern Advaita. Andrew Fort points out that

> Concerning the states, there is an interesting sub-theme which occasionally appears in the *catuṣpād* context: the idea of a "simultaneity doctrine", in which each state simultaneously interpenetrates the others. Śaṅkara pointed out the existence of three states in waking (GK I. 2-3), and Sureśvara subdivides each state three ways in his *BāU bhāṣya-vārttika* IV. 3. 1055ff. Some minor Upaniṣads include sixteen part divisions. Śrī Aurobindo will present, as part of his refutation of Śaṅkara's "illusionism", the idea of interpenetrating "planes of consciousness".[11]

He then goes on to report:

> Swami Veṅkaṭeśānanda presented a "simultaneity doctrine" to me this way: when we talk, the waking state is our verbal discussion, *svapna* is our internal reflection during the conversation, and *suṣupti* is our ignorance of "*turīya* consciousness" at that moment. It is actually rather interesting that more of this type of speculation does not exist. In any event, *turīya* still never becomes "just another state" in this context.[12]

The next point relates to the *turīya* itself. Andrew Fort again notes:

> The conception of deep sleep as serene bliss has important implications for the concept of *turīya*. Gauḍapāda, who sees sleep mainly as ignorance, stresses the role of a fourth "state" beyond sleep. Śaṅkara, on the other hand, emphasizes sleep's pure, blissful nature, thus a "state" beyond (and superior to) which it is difficult to imagine. What remains is the non-dual self, the substratum of states, not itself a state or quarter.
>
> Śaṅkara's exaltation of deep sleep and his equation of *turīya* with the self, seen in the previous chapter, combine to make *turīya* a largely superfluous term for later *Advaitins*. *Turīya* is also avoided because of

its absence from *śruti* and its link with *om* speculation, which is somewhat suspect in Śaṅkara's eyes.[13]

In fact, in later Advaita, attempts to accommodate *turīya within* a scheme of states will lead to what many consider rather artificial formulations.[14]

Sarvajñātmā (c. 900 A.D.) has already been referred to in the course of the discussion of Śaṅkara (as Sarvajñātman), whose conflicting statements of the presence and absence of *avidyā* in dreamless sleep he tried to reconcile. His attempt at a reconciliation of these two positions is carried out on a grander scale than suggested by the earlier reference. The two positions are reflected by the following two contrary propositions:

(1) "For a man in deep sleep, there is no nescience."

(2) "This man in deep sleep was in dense darkness (nescience)."

He argues first for the first position, after stating the two positions in the *Saṁkṣepa-śārīraka*, as follows:

> For a man in deep sleep, there is no nescience. "This man in deep sleep was in dense darkness (nescience)". What is thus stated should be apprehended by you as being without conflict after reflection and through experience and reasoning.
>
> Thus, during deep sleep, there was no nescience at all. In other words, the jīva, indeed, has become the supreme purpose. Because of the absence of relationship (with the causal condition) it (the jīva) has attained to the state of being devoid of the seed (of transmigration); for, here, there is not the clear experience of nescience.
>
> During deep sleep, because of the absence of nescience and its product, viz., the mind, you are the Pure, Supreme, eternally released Lord. At that time, how can desire, activity, and all (their products) be in you who are an ocean of consciousness, who are limitless, and who are perfect?

> There was the egoity produced by your own nescience. It brings in and shows to you extreme misery (and pleasure), while you are awake and while you are in dream. It does not exist during deep sleep, because of the destruction of its seed. Hence it is that you were very pure (during deep sleep).[15]

Then he argues for the second position, as indicating a cosmic fact in relation to the individual.

The wise declare thus:

> This nescience, like the darkness of the night, is admitted to be of the nature of an existent, because of its being experienced as what obscures self-consciousness. Like the sun, knowledge which is of the nature of an inert luminary, is the remover of it (nescience).
>
> By the disputants, too, it should be admitted only thus—(by them) who admit previously non-manifestation in regard to consciousness. Indeed, in regard to consciousness, nescience which is of the nature of the absence of consciousness is not admitted; nor is the absence of *buddhi*.
>
> Consequently, the Upaniṣadic texts and the great sages have stated in various places that it is not conflicting that nescience has the self for its content, nescience which is the single primary cause of the entire world. Hence, there is no conflict. (III.125–131).[16]

This fact that the *jīva* is both with and without nescience will surface again in Advaita and cannot be dissociated from its metaphysical basis, no more than one can say that the snake is or is not in the rope. For the time being the following attempt at clarification must suffice.

> That consciousness of the self which persists in the changing states, viz., waking, dream, deep sleep, swoon, and the extinction of the body—that, indeed, is real. Whatever is changing, is, indeed illusory,

> like garland, serpent, stick, etc. It is impossible to say that the persistent conscious reality, like the rope is illusory.
>
> This *citta*, whose qualities are waking, dream and deep sleep, has arisen from your nescience; hence, it is always you alone. It does not difer from you, your nescience is established on the strength of your experience (and) it is, in fact, illusory. Since it did not, does not, and will not exist (in consciousness), your perfect consciousness (alone) remains. (III.139–140).[17]

Vācaspati Miśra (ninth–tenth century) is an important figure in the development of Advaita Vedānta. In fact he "is considered by many scholars to be one of the most important contributors to Advaita in its post-Śaṅkara phase."[18] And one of his most important contributions in the development of Advatia after Śaṅkara has been the view "that ignorance resides in many different selves, with the *locus* of *avidyā* not being Brahman but the empirical self (*jīva*). Brahman or Ātman is the object (*viṣaya*) of ignorance, but the individual is its locus."[19]

The school of Advaita associated with the name of Vācaspati Miśra is called Bhāmatī. The rival school of Advaita, associated with the name of Padmapāda and others is called Vivaraṇa. There were several differences among the two schools, but in the present context of the role of *suṣupti* in Advaita Vedānta, it would be helpful to identify two such differences and indicate the role the understanding of dreamless sleep may have played in their emergence. With this end in mind the following two differences between the schools may be identified:

(1) According to Vivaraṇa, Brahman-Ātman is the locus of *avidyā*; according to Bhāmatī, the *jīva* is the locus of *avidyā*. The former is often called *brahmāśrita-avidyā-vāda* and the latter *jivāśrita-avidyā-vadā*;

(2) Vivaraṇa is predisposed to a theory of *sṛṣṭi-dṛṣti-vāda* (that the objects of the world exist before and after they are perceived) consistently with its view, that, as the Brahman is the locus of *avidyā*, creation proceeds from it. Bhāmatī is predisposed to a theory of creation called *dṛṣṭi-sṛṣṭi-vāda* (percep-

tion of objects is simultaneous with their creation), which inclines toward subjective idealism, in keeping with its view that, as the *jīva* is the locus of *avidyā*, the *jīva* is actively involved in the manifestation of the world.

The clash between these schools, their differing orientations, and their theoretical positions are adumbrated in the passage that is cited below. In order to appreciate its conclusion and the role the assessment of dreamless sleep plays in it, it is necessary to remind oneself of the standard line about dreamless sleep (*suṣupti*) found in Advaita, which runs as follows: *sukham aham asvāpsam, na kiñcid avediṣam.* 'I slept happily, I did not know anything.'

> Just as the origin of the Sṛṣṭi-Dṛṣṭi-vāda can be reasonably traced back to the Brahmāśrita-avidyā view, enunciated by Padmapāda and Sureśvara, that of the Dṛṣṭi-Sṛṣṭi-vāda also can be detected in the Jīvāśrita-avidyā view, held by Maṇḍana and Vācaspati. Both the Vādas are but the logical developments of the respective views. Contemporary in origin, development and flourishing, these two Vādas,—under which it is quite possible to classify almost all Advaitic thought of the later epoch,—came to a head-long clash, now and then exchanged subtle influences, and moulded each other's development to a considerable extent . . . The apprehensional evidences put forward by the Sṛṣṭi-Dṛṣṭi-vādins to prove the factual existence of the avidyā entity, not only establish what they are adopted for, but also show the real locus of the entity, proved by them. Each and every one of the experiences, such as *'Aham ajñāh'* or *'Sukham aham asvāpsvam, na kiñcidavediṣam,'* clearly points out that it is the individual soul indicated (however erroneously may it be by the notion *'Aham,'* that forms the real locus of *ajñāna*, asserts the Jīvāśrita-avidyā-vādin).[20]

In other words, it is the association of nescience with the state of dreamless sleep of the *jīva*, which is adduced as an argument in favor of the view that the *jīva* is the locus of *avidyā*. Similarly, in order to establish the possibility of *dṛṣṭi-sṛṣṭi-vāda* the followers of this view

> often dwell over the state of suṣupti. Unimpeachable authorities, it is pointed out, emphatically maintain that during the state of suṣupti, where the vision of the individual soul, responsible for all types of erroneous cognitions of diversity of being, lies dormant, there exists no world of diversity as such, independent in its existence. It is because it is non-existent at that time, that it is not apprehended (na tu tat-dvitīyam asti, tatonyat vibhaktam yat paśyet). Thus every time the individual soul enters into the state of suṣupti, the world of diversity, which his apprehension (dṛṣṭi) had conjured up before him during the states of jāgrat and svapna, dissolves away; and every time he wakes out of it, a new world of diversity is presented before him by his vision (dṛṣṭi), active again, thus, there being an ever-new world every morning, the notion of sameness attached to the mutually different members of the world-view-series, obtained by the individual soul, is a wrong notion based on the incapacity to grasp the truth. Now the sole reason behind the factual absence of the world of diversity during the state of suṣupti, can be nothing but the temporary cessation of the conjuring vision of the individual human soul. Owing its emergence and its continuance in being to the latter, the former cannot be existent when the latter is not so. Thus, the abject dependence of the world of diversity on the apprehension thereof has been convincingly established by the negative evidence, offered by the state of suṣupti. Now there is no reason why it should not be accepted in the fields of jagrat and svapna too,—ask the protagonists of . . . Dṛṣṭi-Sṛṣṭi-vāda.[21]

The views of Prakāśātmā (thirteenth century) may be considered next, if only in passing. He belonged to the Vivaraṇa school.[22] His use of the phenomenon of deep sleep as a state simultaneously characterized by the absence of an ego and the presence of pure consciousness possesses considerable clarifying power. In Advaitic terms:

> in dreamless sleep (*suṣupti*) where all the functions of the internal and external organs cease, the Ego (*ahaṅkāra*) cannot shine at all, but the self as Pure Consciousness still shines (cf. the *Śruti atrāyaṁ puruṣaḥ svayaṁjyoti*). In the dreamless sleep, then, Pure Consciousness cannot be said to have been brought to a cessation, for that would mean that Consciousness has left the body by making it, *consiousness-less*—an absurd proposition. In dreamless sleep, what then is actually the state according to the Advaitists. The functions of all the organs being stopped, Pure Consciousness or the Self shines forth in its own light, with the fullness of *avidyā (nescience)* lying passive on it. There is no creation or destruction of knowledge-situations, no rising and falling of the *āvidyaka* or illusory world; the Pure Self alone shines forth as the self-luminous principle as the *mere substratum* of the passive state of all-engrossing *avidyā*.[23]

Vidyāraṇya (fourteenth century), otherwise known as Bharatītīrtha or as Bharartītīrtha-Vidyāraṇya, devotes the eleventh chapter of his well-known work of Advaita, the *Pañcadaśī*, to the discussion of dreamless sleep.[24] The treatment is extended and detailed. Its main points are presented below.

The first major point Vidyāraṇya makes in the context of his discussion of dreamless sleep is that it constitutes an example of *nondual* experience (XI.29). This point is easily made, as it is obvious to all "that there is in sleep no subject at all and no states of consciousness."[25] The next point he makes is that the phenomenon of dreamless sleep also constitutes an example of the *self-luminous* nature of the experience. How is the experience of sleep known? By itself. This "is sufficient proof of the self-revealing nature of this experience of sleep. Knowledge which arises by itself without any cause may be said to shine by its own light."[26] The point to note is that

> In sleep there is not the functioning of the senses. Nor can that experience be established through inference from the sleep of another person. Means of valid knowledge like perception and inference are not able to establish the experience of sleep. But still we cannot but testify to the fact of such an experience; and hence it is self-luminous.[27]

The third point to be established is the blissful nature of dreamless sleep. The point is fairly obvious, though it is established with much circumstance (XI.34–46), and the following examples are given to illustrate the point (XI.46–54):

> The scriptures give the following examples to illustrate the bliss enjoyed in sleep: the falcon, the eagle, the infant; the great king and the knower of Brahman.
>
> Tied to a string, the falcon, flying hither and thither but failing to find a resting place, returns to rest on the wrist of its master or on the post to which it is tied.
>
> Similarly the mind, which is the instrument of the Jīva, moves on in the dreaming and waking states in order to obtain the fruits of righteous and unrighteous deeds. When the experiencing of these fruits ceases, the mind is absorbed in its cause, undifferentiated ignorance.
>
> The eagle rushes only to its nest hoping to find rest there. Similarly the Jiva eager only to experience the bliss of Brahman rushes to sleep.
>
> A tiny tot having fed at the breast of its mother, lies smiling in a soft bed. Free from desire and aversion it enjoys the bliss of its nature.
>
> A mighty king, sovereign of the world, having obtained all the enjoyments which mark the limits of human happiness to his full contentment becomes the very personification of bliss.
>
> A great Brahmana, a knower of Brahman, has extended the bliss of knowledge to its extreme limit; he has achieved all that was to be achieved and sits established in that state.

> These examples of the ignorant, infant, the discriminative king and wise Brahmana are of people considered to be happy. Others are subject to misery and are not very happy.
>
> Like the infant and the other two, man passes into deep sleep and enjoys only the bliss of Brahman. In that state he, like a man embraced by his loving wife, is not conscious of anything either internal or external.

Scriptural testimony is hardly required to confirm the blissful nature of sleep, for it is

> experience of all who say after waking up from sleep: 'Happily did we sleep; we knew nothing in our sleep'. Thus there is the reflective cognition of happiness and nescience which were experienced in sleep. Reflective cognition is grounded in experience, for without the latter the former is not possible. Nor may it be said that since in sleep there are no recognized means of knowledge there can be no experience of happiness and nescience.[28]

The crucial questions that arise at this point are: *who* experiences that bliss and *how* is it experienced? The Advaitin answer *rejects* the explanation of Yoga school and *offers* the explanation consistent with its own physiology and metaphysics. One would be tempted to argue as follows in line with Yoga: "The jīva which has the intellect for adjunct remembers that it slept happily without knowing anything. Since experience and the recognition thereof must have the same locus, the jiva conditioned by the intellect must have experienced happiness and nescience in sleep."[29] This explanation is, however, rejected, and the mainline Advaitin explanation is offered:

> This statement is not valid, for in sleep the intellect and the mind which are the products of nescience get resolved in their cause; and since the adjunct, the in-

> tellect, is non-existent, there cannot be the jīva as conditioned by intellect. *What experienced happiness and nescience in sleep is the anandamaya self, and the remembrance of that by the vijnanamaya self is intelligible because the self is the same in both the states of experience, although the adjuncts may vary.*[30]

What is said to happen is that the "self which assumes many forms in the states of waking and dream becomes a single consistency in sleep; and the intelligence which is reflected in nescience serves as the channel for the enjoyment of bliss."[31] The *ānanadamaya* self enjoys bliss by the "subtle modes of nescience."[32]

It is, of course, the Advaitic claim that this bliss is the bliss of Brahman. But it is not only bliss but ignorance as well that is experienced in sleep. The simpler version of the explanation goes as follows: "In the state of dreamless sleep the Self reveals itself as bliss and in the self-revelation it reveals its knowledge of avidyā or ignorance, which expresses itself as 'I knew nothing.' "[33] Now if it be asked: "How can there be recollection of the bliss and the state of non-duality in deep sleep by the intellect and the mind, for they did not exist?,"[34] the answer offered is that they existed in the latent state in the Ajñāna, their cause, so it is quite possible. They came out of deep sleep with the feeling 'There was abundance in bliss,' 'I did not know anything else.' "[35]

Vidyāraṇya also makes the claim that the bliss experienced by human beings can be of three kinds (XI.87): (1) *Brahmānanda* or "the bliss of Brahman," (2) *Vāsanānanda* or "the bliss arising in the quiescent mind out of the impressions of Brahmānanda" and (3) *Viṣayānanda* or "the bliss resulting from the fulfilment of the desire to be in contact with external objects."[36] Vidyāraṇya then makes the further claim in verses XI.74 that "An examination of the moment immediately succeeding the termination of sleep gives us intimation of the Brahman-bliss experienced during sleep; for there is then the persistence of residual impression of Brahman-bliss which is borne out by the fact that a person who has just got up from sleep remains calm and happy without any thought of external objects."[37] Vidyāraṇya then proceeds to identify this form of bliss with *vāsanānanda*.

At this stage in the discussion it should be indicated that two main points are going to occupy us in the rest of this section: (1) the analysis of bliss by Vidyāraṇya and (2) the role of scriptural authority in this, and, by extension, some similar aspects of Advaita Vedānta.

Vidyāraṇya claims in XI.89: "The fact that the bliss of Brahman is self-revealing in deep sleep is established by the authority of the scriptures, by reasoning, and by one's experience."

The existence of bliss during dreamless sleep seems like a reasonable and acceptable premise; and it also is not past reason that it may be called self-revealing in the sense that there was no empirical consciousness operating in sleep to reveal it, yet the experience cannot be denied and may therefore be accepted as self-revealing. But to claim that such bliss is the bliss of Brahman is clearly a dogmatic claim. One's reasoning and experience do establish a case of nondual self-luminous state of bliss in deep sleep—but there seems to be no way of connecting it with the experience of ultimate reality except *through* scripture.

Once this connection is made, Vidyāraṇya has a fairly interesting theory of the experience of bliss. It may be summarized as follows:

> So far we have seen how there is the experience of Brahman-bliss in the state of sleep, how it is self-luminous and non-dual, as also how there is the indication of the bliss immediately prior to sleep, and an intimation thereof in the form of residual impression immediately subsequent to sleep. The happiness which is the result of the residual impression of bliss is experienced whenever there is happiness which is not due to the objects of the external world. This is what we have called vāsanānanda. What is known as *viṣayānanda* is the reflection of bliss in the mental mode which has turned inward after the desire for external objects is destroyed through attaining them. As was remarked above, the latter two kinds of bliss are but products of Brahman-bliss, vāsanānanda being its

> reflection in the modes which cognize objects of sense. Both the latter kinds of bliss point towards their generator, viz., Brahman-bliss.[38]

The theory presents a basic problem, what I would call overreliance on scripture. *Not only is the identification of deep sleep bliss with Brahman bliss based on scriptural authority, the subsequent bliss felt on waking up is also to be accepted as a reflection of Brahman-bliss on scriptural authority.*

> We observed above that in the state of calmness there is the manifestation of *Brahman*-bliss in the form of residual impression. Now, since the manifestation of *Brahman*-bliss is obtained in the state of calmness the need for the teaching of scripture and the preceptor may be questioned. The declarations of śruti can be meaningful only when it connotes something which is not established by any other means. This objection is not sound. A man who does not know a piece of precious stone to be such finds no use for it. Even so, although everyone experiences *Brahman*-bliss or residual impression thereof without the help of scripture and the preceptor.[39]

It seems to me that two distinct points need to be made clearly and separately here. The first pertains to scriptural authority in general. I think there is an as yet undetected tension in Advaita, and more so in later Advaita, between *anubhava* and *śruti* as *pramāṇas*. *Anubhava* is arguably accepted by Śaṅkara as a *pramāṇa* and Brahman, being an everpresent reality, should be capable of being directly experienced, yet in the intellectual formulation of Advaita considerable emphasis is laid on Vedic authority. It seems to me that this emphasis, when faced with the fact of experience, tends to degenerate into a kind of nominalism. This is illustrated by the example on hand. One experiences the bliss of Brahman in dreamless sleep but does not *know* that it is the bliss of Brahman till the scriptures tell it to be so! A more significant example is provided by mystical experience.

> As the mystics themselves admit, while in a trance a mystic does not know what he is experiencing; but after coming out of the trance, he interprets his experience in terms of his beliefs. St. Theresa has said: 'How can a person, who is incapable of sight and hearing, know these things—that it has been in God and God in it? I reply that she (the soul) does not see them at the time, but sees them clearly later, after she has returned to herself, and knows them not by vision, but by a certitude which remains in the heart'. Śaṅkara himself says the same.[40]

It is conceivable that one may realize the ultimate reality by oneself. Then one learns from the scriptures that what one realized is Brahman—just as Ramaṇa realized, after his realization, that what he realized was Ātman. Therefore Ramaṇa can declare:

> No learning or knowledge of scriptures is necessary to know the Self, as no man requires a mirror to know that he is himself. All knowledge is acquired only to be given up eventually as not-Self. Nor is household work or care of children necessarily an obstacle. If you can do nothing more, at least continue saying 'I' 'I' to yourself mentally all the time, whatever work you may be doing and whether you are sitting, standing or walking. 'I' is the name of God. It is the first and greatest of all mantras.
>
> Even OM is second to it.[41]

Now Ramaṇa as a child was a very heavy sleeper, and this may strengthen the case for a closer connection between the experience of deep sleep and Brahman. But the point I wish to make is not that scriptural insights may not be corroborated, or that spiritual insights may not be generated by scriptural statements[42] or that we might know otherwise.[43] All I wish to say is that by placing an *overemphasis* on scripture, the tradition was at times reduced to making merely verbal accommodations to maintain the fiction of its authority.

The second point is that the relationship between experience and scripture need not be antithetical and can even be positive. Like the Englishman who was surprised to learn that he had been speaking prose for forty years, we may be surprised to learn that the transcendental Brahman may be more familiar to us as a matter of experience than we realize. In this respect the experience of deep sleep can be helpful as an analogy, if we are prepared to bite at the Advaitic bait. An interesting illustration of this is provided by the *Tripurā Rahasya*, wherein we are told that Samādhic moments in normal living go unnoticed because we do not connect them with the phenomenon of Samādhi. The text provides a pertinent and telling example: *"Men when they are awake can detect fleeting sleep because they are already conversant with its nature."*[44]

Attention also needs to be paid to Vidyāraṇya's views on the relationship between sleep and *samādhi*. In this context his position may be summarized as follows: (1) the mind as it exists in *samādhi* is in a state superior to which it is found in sleep[45] and (2) not surprisingly, sleep as a state is inferior to *samādhi*.[46] As for praxis:

> Vidyāraṇya goes on to make an interesting comment about meditation practice and sleep, following Gauḍapāda's linking of sleep and destruction (laya) (GK III.42–6). He points out that when one turns away from objects by *samādhi* practice, the mind resists and tries to go to sleep. One now continually struggles to stay awake and suppress the urge to sleep, for work on "awakening" is fatiguing. He concludes that when practising meditation intensively, one should be sure to get enough sleep, eat moderately those things which are easily digested, and remain in a restful atmosphere.[47]

The *Vedāntasāra* of Sadānanda (sixteenth century) is a popular text of Advaita Vedānta. The discussion of *suṣupti* or dreamless sleep is particularly interesting therein because it is carried on in the context of *māyā*. Its views on *māyā* need to be ascertained first to gauge the full significance of its location of the self, when in deep sleep, in the general scheme of things in Advaita. He maintains that *māyā* could be viewed either singly or collectively.

> This Ignorance is treated as one or as multiplex, according as it is regarded as a collective or distributive aggregate. Just as, when regarding a collection of trees as a whole, we speak of them as one thing, namely, a forest; or as, when regarding a collection of waters as a whole, we call them a lake, so when we look at the aggregate of the ignorances residing in individual souls and seeming to be manifold, we regard them as one. As it is said in the Veda, "[The one, unborn, individual soul approaches] the one, unborn (Prakriti)."[48]

Sadānanda adopts the aggregative approach to the issue first.

> This collective aggregate [or ignorances], having as its associate (upādhi) that which is most excellent, abounds in pure goodness. Intelligence associated with it, having the qualities of omniscience, omnipotence, and universal control, indiscrete, is called the internal ruler, the cause of the world, and Īśvara; because it is the illuminator of the whole of Ignorance. As the Veda says, "Who knows all [generally], who knows everything [particularly]."
>
> This totality [of ignorance], being the cause of all things, is Īśvara's causal body. It is also called 'the sheath of bliss,' because it is replete with bliss, and envelops all things like a sheath; and 'dreamless sleep,' because everything reposes in it,—on which account it is also regarded as the scene of the dissolution of all subtle and gross bodies."[49] This is then complemented by the distributive approach "As, when regarding a forest as a distributive aggregate of trees, there is a perception of its manifoldness, which is also perceived in the case of a lake regarded as a distributive aggregate of waters,—so, when viewing Ignorance distributively, we perceive it to be multiplex. As the Veda says, "Indra, by his supernatural powers, appears multiform."[50]

Thus, then, a thing is regarded as a collective or distributive aggregate according as it is viewed as a whole or as a collection of parts.

> Distributive ignorance, having a humble associate, abounds in impure goodness. Intelligence associated with it, having the qualities of parviscience and parvipotence, is called Prājña, owing to its being the illuminator of one Ignorance only. The smallness of its intelligence is because its illuminating power is limited by its associate's want of clearness.
>
> This [distributive Ignorance] is the individual's causal body, because it is the cause of the making of 'I,' etc. It is also called 'the sheath of bliss', because it abounds in bliss and covers like a sheath; and 'dreamless sleep,' because all things repose in it,—on which account it is said to be the scene of the dissolution of the subtle and gross body.[51]

The striking result that is achieved by adopting these approaches is the equation of *prājña* or the self in dreamless sleep on the micro scale with Īśvara or God on the macro scale.[52]

It seems that the parallel has to be understood carefully. And the remarks must be examined with caution. There seems to be a good case for instituting a comparison between the state of dreamless sleep (*suṣupti*) of the individual and the condition of Īśvara, when in the case of Īśvara "this refers to the state of dissolution (*pralaya*)."[53] But from the *Chāndogya* text cited by Swami Nikhilananda it is claimed that "we learn that in dreamless sleep the *jīva* becomes united with *Īśvara*."[54] This direct identification could be problematical. The relevant text itself does not seem to say so:

> In the state of dreamless sleep both Ishwara and Prajna, through a very subtle function of ignorance illumined by Consciousness, enjoy happiness, as in the shruti passage: 'Prajna, the enjoyer of bliss, with Consciousness for its aid (is the third aspect)' (Mand. Up. 5); as

> also from such experience of a man awaking from dreamless sleep as, 'I slept happily, I did not know anything.'[55]

While it may be true that a parallel has been drawn between the two, the parallel has its limits. The limit arises out of the difference between the individual and God in relation to *avidyā* or *māyā*. In *nuce,* God is the wielder of *māyā,* but the individual is a yielder of *avidyā*. However, adopting the author's own dual approach one could say either that Īśvara "forms the cosmic parallel of the individual self or ego. Each is Brahman itself with an unreal adjunct; only the adjunct is *all-comprehensive* in one case, while it is finite in the other,"[56] or that we must not think of Īśvara that "he is deluded"[57] in the control of nescience, that nescience is not under his control.[58]

The text quoted by Sadānananda is no doubt Upaniṣadic. *Māṇḍūkya* 6 declares of the *Prājña*: "This is the lord of all; this is the knower of all, this is the inner controller; this is the source of all; this is the beginning and the end of things."[59]

However, as Śaṅkara points out, "that which is designated as *prājña* (when it is viewed as the cause of the world) will be described as *turīya* separately when it is not viewed as the cause, and when it is free from all phenomenal relationship i.e., in its absolute real aspect."[60]

The point to be realized here is that if one stops short now, one may miss the real point—that the comparison needs to be carried a step further. As S. Radhakrishnan points out:

> It is the first time in the history of thought that the distinction between Absolute and God, Brahman and vara, *turīya* and *prājña* is elaborated. Cp. with this the Christian view of the Son as 'the image of the invisible God, the first born of all creation; for in him all things were created, in heaven and on earth, visible and invisible . . . all things were created through him and for him. He is before all things and in his all things hold together'. Colossians I.15. The son is the Demiurge, the heavenly architect, not the God but the image of the God. For Philo 'the Sun itself unaffected

> and undiminished by its radiance, yet all the earth is dependent on it; so God, although in His being He is completely self-contained and self-sufficient, shoots forth a great stream of radiation, immaterial, yet on that account all the more real. This stream is God in extension, God in relation, the son of God, not God.'[61]

This elaboration, based on the discussion of the sleep in the *Vedāntasāra*,

> illustrates the intimate relation between *bandhutā* homologies and this doctrine. The *samaṣṭi* characteristics are added to the 'basic' homologies in the *Māṇḍūkya* and some effort is made to explicate the connections. Sadānanda also takes the states of consciousness aspect seriously, holding to the *Advaita* conception of a substratum underlying changing states. He emphasizes that *turīya* is *caitanya* in its pure form. *Caitanya*, in fact seems to be the central concept for Sadānanda, playing the role which the self plays for Śaṅkara. Once again we find *turīya* linked with another, more central, concept, rather than standing on its own.[62]

Vedāntaparibhāṣā is also a popular manual of Advaita Vedānta, which was composed by Dharmarāja, also known as Dharmarājādhvarīndra, in the seventeenth century.[63] Although its treatment of Advaita Vedānta is primarily devoted to epistemology, other aspects of Advaita are also covered.

The discussion of dreamless sleep in the *Vedāntaparibhāṣā* occurs in two distinct contexts. It is first discussed in the context of *pralaya*[64] or dissolution and then again discussed in the context of the meaning of the word *tvam* in the *mahāvākya: tat tvam asi*, in relation to the individual self in the three states of wakefulness, dream, and deep sleep.[65]

Both the discussions help advance our understanding of dreamless sleep in Advaita Vedānta. It is important to note at this point that *suṣupti* or the state of dreamless sleep, in which "a person is like dead to the world" is "known metaphorically as daily death (*dainandina maraṇam*)."[66] This description raises an interesting problem, as according to Advaita, *prāṇa* (or breath) and *citta* (or mind) originate from the same source. In dreamless sleep, however, the mind is held to be in abeyance but breathing continues, a situation that obviously requires an adequate explanation, if the linkage between the two is to be insisted upon. This issue is among those addressed in the following passage:

> Now cosmic dissolution is being described. It is the destruction of the world in general. It is of four kinds—diurnal, basic, occasional and absolute. Of these, diurnal (nitya) dissolution is the condition of profound sleep, for it represents the dissolution of all effects. Merit, demerit and past latent impressions then remain in their causal form. Hence, for a person awaking from sleep, pleasure, pain, etc. are not incongruous; nor is recollection inexplicable. In profound sleep, though the mind is destroyed, yet the function of respiration etc., which depend on that, are not incongruous, because, though really there are no respiration, etc., yet their cognition is just phantasy of another person, like the cognition of the body of a sleeping man. It cannot be urged that in that case a sleeping man would be indistinguishable from a dead man; for there is this distinction that the subtle body of a sleeping man remains here itself in the form of latent impressions, while that of a dead man remains in another world.[67]

According to this view the main distinction between the sleeping man and the dead man is the presence of the subtle body *within* the sleeping man and its absence in the case of the dead body. The fact of respiration, played down above, is accorded greater importance in the next passage:

> Or (we may say) the mind has two functions—the functions of knowledge and that of activity. Of these, the mind as possessed of the function of knowledge is destroyed in profound sleep, but not the mind as possessed of the function of activity. Hence the conti-

> nuity of the vital force etc. is not contradictory. Śruti texts like the following are proofs of the above condition of profound sleep: "When a person is asleep and sees no dreams, he verily becomes one with (Brahman associated with) this vital force. Then the organ of speech with all names merge in It: (Kau. IV.19), "He is then united with Existence, my dear—is merged in his Self" (Cha. Vi.viii.1).[68]

This explanation coheres better than the one Ramaṇa Maharshi was to offer later: "The scriptures however say that the *prāṇa* protects the body in sleep. For when the body lies on the floor, a wolf or a tiger may feed on it. The animal sniffs and feels that there is life within and therefore does not feed on it as a corpse. That again shows that there is someone in the body to protect it in deep sleep."[69] The explanation of knowledge and breathing as psychological and physiological functions has a certain neatness to it and no appeal to "divine law" is required.[70]

Dharmarāja discusses the question of dreamless sleep again in relation to the three states of consciousness.

> The dream condition is that in which illusory objects are immediately cognised by a mental state that is not caused by the organs. The clause, "That is not caused by the organs," is for excluding the waking condition. In order to guard against the definition unwarrantedly including profound sleep, which has a state of nescience, the word 'mental' has been inserted. Profound sleep is that condition in which a state of nescience has nescience for its object. Since the state resembling nescience in the waking condition and dream is a mental state, the definition does not unwarrantedly include them. Regarding this some say that death and swoon are other conditions. Others, however, maintain that they are included in profound sleep. Now as their inclusion in the three conditions or exclusion from them has no bearing on the ascertainment of the meaning of the word 'thou,' no attempt is being made to deal with it.[71]

This passage is of interest because it departs from the more traditional Advaitin explanations at some points. The explanation of deep sleep is in the main orthodox, when it is described as "a condition in which a state of nescience has nescience as its object," as in saying "I know nothing," my ignorance has ignorance as its object. The more formal explanation runs as follows: "A man waking from sleep says, 'I slept happily, I knew nothing'. This recollection of the natural bliss of the self as also of ignorance is a proof that in profound sleep nescience only functions, not the mind; and the object of that immediate modification of nescience is also nescience."[72]

But Dharmarāja's presentation contains elements of novelty in two ways. (1) Dharmarāja regards dreams as mental modifications. Here, in Madhavananda's opinion, "the author seems to differ from the general view that in dreams there are no mental modifications, but only modifications of nescience."[73] But a subsequent comment indicates that there is room for a revised assessment: "What is called sleep is a state of nescience psychosis (transformation) having nescience (constant blissfulness of sleep) for its sphere. Since the psychoses [involved are] (transformations) of the internal organ (primarily, and of nescience, only indirectly), there is no overpervasion of these."[74] Another scholar however identifies Dharmarāja's position unequivocally as follows: "Deep sleep is a mode of nescience, which apprehends the nescience. In this state the internal organ is merged in nescience, and so has no mode, but nescience has a mode which apprehends it."[75] (2) We noted earlier the elaborate discussion in Śaṅkara on the nature of swoon in relation to deep sleep. Dharmarāja, however, is interested in explaining the "Thou" or *tvam* part of the great saying "that thou art" (*tat tvam asi*). He is able to sweep aside the issue of death, swoon, etc. and their relation to deep sleep, by maintaining that as their inclusion or exclusion in the normally tribasic states of consciousness has no bearing on the ascertainment of the meaning 'thou,' no attempt is being made to deal with them. Dharmarāja's position is interesting inasmuch as it succeeds in problematizing an issue in the first instance and deproblematizing it in the other.

The foregoing discussion may be supplemented by taking two other texts into account which, though not strictly in the Advaitic tradition, cannot be totally isolated by it. One is the *Yogavāsiṣṭha* and the other is the *Paramārthasāra*.

The *Yogavāsiṣṭha* is a text difficult to date. It has been assigned as early as to the ninth and as late as the thirteenth century. It could accommodate both the dates, if viewed as taking shape during this time frame by stages.

> The work bears the strong imprint of Gauḍapāda's thought. Thus section *Utpatti* 22 concurs with Gauḍapāda's view that waking and dream 'bodies' are equally unreal, although the dream body is more subtle. *Suṣupti* is said to be sleep (*nidrā*) with dormant impressions (*suptavāsanā*), while *turīya* is sleep with the impressions completely destroyed. *Pūrvanirvāṇa* 128. 49–51 asserts that when non-duality is seen, the liberated self enters the bliss of *turīya*, abandoning the states which have sleep as seed (*bījanidrā*, GK I. 13).[76]

In this context Andrew Fort refers to two other sections, one which is "most akin to Gauḍapāda" and another where "one is reminded of Śaṅkara as well as Gauḍapāda."[77] The point then is that the legacy of both Gauḍapāda and Śaṅkara in relation to sleep continued to be influential even outside strictly Advaitic circles.

The other text, the *Paramārthasāra* is the work of Abhinavagupta (tenth century),[78] for which a text of the same name by Ādiśeṣa may have served as a prototype.[79] The remarks made in verses 34–35 of this text bear on sleep.

> In 34, the author writes that creation-persistence-cessation and waking-dreaming-deep sleep are revealed (*bhā*) in the fourth condition (*dhāma*); however, *turīya* is itself revealed (only when) not covered (*āvṛt*) by them. Verse 35 adds that waking is *viśva* due to difference, dream is *tejas* due to the magnitude (*māhātmya*) of illumination (*prakāśa*), and sleep is *prājña* due to "massedness"

> (*ghanatva*) of knowledge; *turīya* however is beyond that (*tataḥ paraṁ turīyam*). There is no mention of states after these verses, as Abhinavagupta goes on to discuss the path to union with *Śiva*.[80]

Once again we have evidence here of Advaitic views on sleep percolating into Hindu thought in general.

6

Sleep in Modern Advaita

I

The discussion of the phenomenon of deep sleep takes on a new texture in modern Advaita. This is so on account of the fact that while the literature of premodern Advaita combines both intellectual and mystical elements almost inextricably, and often in the same exponent of the tradition, it becomes possible to distinguish between exponents of modern Advaita on the basis of the preponderance of the one or the other. However, although we may now distinguish between an intellectual or academic type of an exponent more clearly from the mystical, one should not assume that the other element is totally absent. In fact the two are arguably combined in almost equal measure in a figure such as Aurobindo (1872–1950). In the case of the analysis of deep sleep offered by such an academic philosopher as Krishnachandra Bhattacarya (1875–1949) on the one hand and a sagely figure such as Ramaṇa Maharshi (1879–1950) on the other, however, it might be possible to argue that the intellectual element may be considered predominant in the exposition of the former, and the mystical element in the exposition of the latter. One might also use this occasion to distinguish between an academic philosopher such as Krishnachandra Bhattacarya and an intellectual philosopher such as Aurobindo, without implying that the former lacked the quality of an intellectual or the latter the potential of being an academic. The difference is vocational more than anything else.

The foregoing discussion implies that in discussing deep sleep in modern Advaita we possess a unique kind of source material hitherto not available to us—namely, the firsthand account of what an Advaitic mystic such as Ramaṇa Maharshi has to say about it. It is true that primary material of this kind has not been altogether lacking, and some sections of the *Upaniṣads* actually seem to come quite close to offering accounts of firsthand experience. Nevertheless I think it might still be permissible to maintain that the amount and clarity in which it is now available, as in the case of a modern mystic like Ramaṇa or Aurobindo, far exceeds anything comparable from ancient or even medieval times.

With these initial observations one might then proceed to review the role of the state of deep sleep in modern Advaita. These initial observations also seem to indicate a natural order in the way such a review might be presented. One could begin with the analysis of deep sleep offered by the academic philosopher Krishnachandra Bhattacharya, followed by that of the intellectual mystic Aurobindo. One could conclude with an analysis of deep sleep in Advaita as offered by Ramaṇa Maharshi.

II

In order to present the thought of Krishnachandra Bhattacharya (1875–1949),[1] a major modern Advaita thinker,[2] on the philosophical significance of deep sleep, it might be helpful to begin by identifying the main strands in this connection as found in Upaniṣadic and classical Advaita as follows:

(1) In the *Upaniṣads,* when the search for the Self takes an inward turn, each state of consciousness is said to correspond to a certain concept of self, ultimately leading to the identification of the Self or *ātman.*[3]

(2) The presence of such an abiding Self is identified not merely in the states of consciousness experienced in the course of one life usually as waking, dreaming, and deep sleep but also in the passage from one life to another. Thus the *Chāndogya Upaniṣad* (VIII. 7–12) "affirms the doctrine that that which remains constant in all the vicissitudes of life viz., of waking, dream and sleep, death, rebirth and deliverance is the persisting spirit."[4] It is significant therefore, that the states of waking, dreaming, and deep sleep are connected with the *sthūla, sūkṣma,* and *kāraṇa śārīra*, the process of transmigration is connected with the concept of a *liṅga-śarīra* and just as the Self, as connected with the three states of consciousness is described successively as *vaiśvānara, taijasa,* and *prājña* in the *Māṇḍūkya Upaniṣad*, it is described in the context of experiencing death, rebirth, and deliverance as *jīva*.

(3) The emphasis on the Self is important, and consequently on deep sleep as an experience of the Self, because as Śaṅkara points out in the course of his commentary on the *Kaṭha Upaniṣad* (II.1.3) "the self cannot manifest itself as an object for it is present in all experiences of the self."[5]

(4) On account of the "apparent absence of duality" in the experience of deep sleep, which approximates the nondualistic stance of the Advaita, deep sleep was "sometimes regarded as the final state of union with *Brahman*,"[6] (as in *Chāndogya Upaniṣad* VIII.12.1).[7]

(5) The state of deep sleep however needs to be distinguished from the *Brahman*-experience. One way of doing this would be to follow Śaṅkara's comment on *Sāṅkya-kārikā* (IV.88) that the ultimate experience is "beyond all empirical experiences. All empirical experiences consist of the subject-object relationship."[8] In deep sleep one experiences the absence of the object and is therefore not free of this relationship. In the ultimate experience even the "consciousness of this absence is absent."[8A]

Krishnachandra Bhattacharya approaches the study of deep sleep as a state of consciousness in the same spirit as the *Upaniṣads*, namely that the analysis of the psychological states is carried out to yield metaphysical conclusions. The manner in which he goes about this, however, is different.

The key distinction Bhattacharya operates with in this context is the distinction between presentation and representation. In the waking state the objects are both physically presented, as well as mentally represented. In other words, while without "sensation there cannot be consciousness in the waking state, but in dreams 'the ideas, or perceptions do not consciously remember the corresponding waking percepts; they are at once percepts without sensation or reference to sensation.' "[9]

In other words, the ideas have become, to a remarkable extent, freed from objects in the sense of no longer remaining tied to them, as in the waking state. In this respect the dream state is "freer" compared to the waking state. According to Bhattacharya, the fact that this state is not constrained by the spatio-temporal regularities of the waking state is further proof of such freedom. In fact Bhattacharya distinguishes between a "merely conscious dream" and a "self-conscious dream," in that in the former 'each isolated image is turned into a percept'[10] while in the latter the Self "seems to create freely *its* world, *its* space and time"[11] so as, for instance, to be able to see "the whole of space as one function."[12] However,

> In spite of this freedom, we find a regularity in the combination of images in self-conscious dream. This fact leads to the truth of the existence of a self-conscious entity behind the mental stages. According to Bhattacharya this entity though unconscious is self-conscious.
>
> He points out that in deep sleep there is a twofold direct consciousness of (i) the absence of the knowledge and (ii) the absence of disquiet i.e. blissful sleep. This awareness in a man waking from sleep can be accounted for only by memory, which in turn needs the presentation (or existence) of the two phenomena in question. It is not something inferred from the memory of our states before and after sleep. We cannot infer or know anything that is not presented. We have the awareness now of the two factors because they were presented in deep sleep. In the case of negative concepts the general principle that ideas should

> have their corresponding percepts is not valid. However in some way or other we have to presuppose percepts in the above-mentioned case because the two 'absences' cannot be inferred, or referred to unless they are objects of a direct consciousness which is present during the time of self-conscious dream.[13]

According to Bhattacharya:

> From the above argument certain central concepts of *Vedānta* philosophy with regard to the self and knowledge evolve. If we ask what is the self in the above context *Vedānta* would say "self is the breath (life spirit) of this knowledge, the light of consciousness, something eternally accomplished rather than being accomplished." Then what is knowledge in that context? "Knowledge, according to *vedānta*," writes Bhattacharya, "is not only different from the knowing activity, it cannot even be described as the (contingent) result of the activity." Its essential character is its eternality, its self-manifestation (*svayaṁ-prakāsatvā*).
>
> This identical view of the self and knowledge leads us to the conclusion that the Self or *Brahman* is the perception turned into an apparently processless accomplished cognition, or pure consciousness.[14]

Bhattacharya's analysis of deep sleep thus presents both points of continuities and discontinuities with the premodern approach to it. Kurian T. Kadankavil maintains that Bhattacharya's analysis of the states of consciousness

> accepted the following concepts as established truths:
>
> (i) the gradation of existence,
>
> (ii) grades of subjectivity,
>
> (iii) the transformation of each grade into the higher one,

(iv) the concept of negative attention,

(v) the belief in a higher grade of existence which would help one to transcend the lower grades.[15]

All of these concepts are consistent with standard Advaitic analysis of the three states of consciousness and the role of deep sleep in the analysis. He breaks fresh ground however in developing the idea of a self-conscious dream, which phenomenologically anticipates the current interest in lucid dreams.

Śrī Aurobindo (1872–1950) is a major modern thinker, who, while disavowing adherence to classical Advaita, does not disdain to use its categories, albeit charging them with new significance. Thus, although he is not a modern Advaitin as such, his treatment of sleep may not be without relevance to the discussion of sleep in Advaita Vedānta. In order to appreciate his contribution to the subject on hand, it might help to begin by first noticing the ways in which the overall template of his thought differs from that of Advaita Vedānta.

Śrī Aurobindo accuses Śaṅkara of "illusionism" and therefore tries to differentiate his more 'realistic' Advaita from Śaṅkara's illusionistic Advaita. What this means in terms of sleep is that, whereas Śaṅkara emphasizes the *radical discontinuity* between the substratum and the three states (including sleep) which it underlies, Aurobindo is more inclined to see an *evolutionary continuity* connecting them. Thus, according to him, the "fourfold scale" found in the *Māṇḍūkya Upaniṣad* "corresponds to the degrees of the ladder by which we climb back towards the absolute Divine,"[16] rather than just fall away from it. Nor is it surprising that once one begins to think of the 'states,' akin to those of Advaita, on a grander scale, they can be construed as "planes" of "superconscient and subliminal" consciousness. Moreover, once these states and planes are viewed as more interactive in nature, the appreciation of deep sleep accordingly changes. Deep sleep (*suṣupti*) could then be described more cosmically as

> a state of spirit less unknowable . . . in which the conceptions of finity and division pre-exist in a potential state. [It]

> is called variously Avyakta, the unmanifestation or the seed condition, or the condition of absolute sleep, because as yet phenomena and activity are not manifest but pre-exist gathered together and undeveloped.[17]

Similarly, the state of dreaming (or *svapna*) can also be reconfigured cosmically as

> the psychical condition of Spirit [which] operates in a world of subtle matter finer and more elastic than gross physical matter, and therefore not subject to the heavy restrictions and slow processes with which the latter is burdened. [Dream is also the] Garbha, Embroyon, because out of psychical matter physical life and form are selected and evolved into the final or Waking-State in which Spirit manifests itself as physically visible, audible, and sensible form and life.[18]

However, when an overall comparison between the two systems is instituted, it is the similarities between the two rather than the differences on the question of deep sleep that appear more significant. Andrew O. Fort explains:

> I would argue that the differences between Aurobindo and Śaṅkara regarding the *catuṣpād* doctrine are less fundamental than Aurobindo would like us to think. Both accept the MāU distinction between gross waking "matter" and subtle dream "matter", and both see sleep as the luminous seed condition. Aurobindo's "superconscience" could, in fact, be a modern approximation of the concept of *saṁprasāda*. Śaṅkara's description of the simultaneous existence of the other states in waking (GK I. 2–3) is similar to the idea of interpenetrating planes. Finally, while Śaṅkara says that the three states are unreal (*asatya*) to the highest view, Aurobindo surely oversimplifies when he asserts that Śaṅkara "negates" the states.
>
> Thus, Aurobindo's "planes of consciousness" interpretation seems basically consistent with the MāU/

> *Advaita* conception. He takes waking and dream relatively more seriously than does Śaṅkara, but both stress the "supramental" aspect of sleep and "*ātmatva* of *turīya*." Aurobindo's language might also contribute to the apparent contrast.[19]

The views of some other modern "Advaitins," a few of whom he interviewed, on sleep are summarized by Andrew O. Fort as follows:

> Two . . . (Vidyānanda, Brahmānanda) held that sleep was blissful; they also said that sleep retained unmanifest *vṛttis*, although no manifest ones such as those which appear in waking and dream. Swami Brahmānanda (in *Revelation of Ever-Revealed* [Shivanandanagar: Divine Life Society, 1978], p. 207 ff.) added that "ignorance" in sleep was not due to *avidyā*, but to oneness with brahman wherein no particularized knowledge is possible. Other swamis did not mention deep sleep or gave perfunctory responses to my questions, and the term *samprasāda* never arose.[20]

Despite differences in nuance it is clear that the experience of deep sleep retains its appeal and is appealed to by modern thinkers in the Advaitic mold. The following excerpt of a conversation between Swami Krishnananda of the Divine Life Society (founded by Swami Shivananda), and Sarah, is instructive in this regard. The context is provided by the search for one's "ontological" foundation:

> *Sarah:* So I have to look within myself to find it.
>
> *Swamiji:* Go deep, deeper than what you seem to be. What is inside the body? You will find the mind. What is inside the mind? Intellect. What is inside the intellect? In deep sleep, the body is not there, the mind is not there, the intellect is not there. But are you there? In deep sleep, are you there, or are you not there?

Sarah: It is both.

Swamiji: You are there. Have you a doubt? Are you existing in the state of deep sleep, or are you not existing?

Sarah: I do not know. It seems like it is both,—that one is all existence, ultimate existence.

Swamiji: Are you alive or dead in deep sleep?

Sarah: Very alive.

Swamiji: How do you know that you are alive? Who told you?
When you had no consciousness of your existence in sleep, how do you make a statement that you are alive there? It is a hearsay, or real fact? Now you are stumbling on something which is the mystery of your being. That which you were in the state of deep sleep is your real personality—not intellect, not mind, not the senses, not the body, not relations, not friends, not enemies, not gold, not silver. Without anything you existed, and let us know what it was that existed at that time. That is your ontological status, the answer to your question.[21]

To follow the main trend of Advaitic thought in modern Advaita regarding deep sleep, however, one may now turn to Ramaṇa Maharshi.[22]

Ramaṇa Maharshi (1879–1950) is a modern Advaitin who constantly alludes to the phenomenon of deep sleep in his discourses. He was therefore naturally asked to explain or define sleep. This sometimes led to a standoff, as, for instance, in the following case:

An Andhra visitor asked: What is sleep?

M.: Why, you experience it every day.

D.: I want to know exactly what it is, so that it may be distinguished from samadhi.

M.: How can you know sleep when you are awake? The answer is to go to sleep and find out what it is.

D.: But I cannot know it in this way.

M.: This question must be raised in sleep.

D.: But I cannot raise the question then.

M.: So, that is sleep.[23]

A similar problem arose with a Muslim visitor, who was presumably even less familiar with the philosophical significance attached to sleep in Hinduism.

A Moulvi asked: How does sleep overtake one?

M.: If the enquirer knows who is awake in the wakeful condition he will also know how sleep comes on. The enquiry arises only to the waking man and not to the sleeper. It must be easier to know the waking Self than the sleeping Self.

D.: I know how I awoke. But I do not know how sleep comes on. I am aware of my wakeful state. For instance if any one takes away my stick I prevent his doing so, whereas I cannot do so in sleep or in dream. The proof of wakefulness is evident. But what is the proof of sleep?

M.: Your ignorance is the evidence of sleep: your awareness is that of wakefulness.

D.: My wakefulness is known by the opening of my eye. But how does sleep overtake me?

M.: In the same way as sleep overtakes you, wakefulness overtakes you.

D.: But I do not perceive how sleep comes on in the same way as I know my wakefulness.

M.: Never mind.

D.: Please describe what is sleep, without illustrations. Sleep by itself should be known. I want a real picture of sleep.

M.: Such picture is sleep itself.[24]

It seems that Ramaṇa was keen to establish the experiential nature of deep sleep in the mind of the inquirer, as a state which bore the stamp of one's personal experience and and did not require either someone else's, or one's own logic, or outside authority, to establish its reality.

> As Sri Bhagavan was continuing in the same strain, a visitor asked how to overcome the identity of the Self with the body.
>
> M.: What about sleep?
>
> D.: There is ignorance prevailing.
>
> M.: How do you know your ignorance in sleep? Did you exist in sleep, or not?
>
> D.: I do not know.
>
> M.: Do you deny your existence in sleep?
>
> D.: I must admit it by my reasoning.
>
> M.: How do you infer your existence?
>
> D.: By reasoning and experience.
>
> M.: Is reasoning necessary for experience? (Laughter)[25]

When this was not the issue—namely, it's *experiential* recognition, he did offer descriptions and explanations of *suṣupti*. These seem to be largely in line with the Advaita tradition. Even then pragmatic concerns were never far from his mind, as the following exchange illustrates "D.: What does *suṣupti* look like? M.: In a cloudy dark night no individual identification of objects is possible and there is only dense darkness, although the seer has his eyes wide open; similarly in *suṣupti* the seer is aware of simple nescience."[26]

On another occasion, he offered an explanation quite consistent with the explanation of deep sleep in later Advaita.

> D.: How are we in sleep?
>
> M.: Ask the question is sleep. You recall the experience of sleep only when you are awake. You recall that state by saying "I slept happily."
>
> D.: What is the instrument by which we experience that state?
>
> M.: We call it *Māyākaraṇa* as opposed to the *antaḥkaraṇa* to which we are accustomed in our other

states. The same instruments are called differently in the different states, even as the *ānandātman* of sleep is termed the *vijñānātman* of the wakeful state.

D.: Please furnish me with an illustration for the *Māyākaraṇa* experiencing the *ānanda*.

M.: How can you say "I slept happily"? The experience is there to prove your happiness. There cannot be the remembrance in the wakeful state in the absence of the experience in the sleep state.

D.: Agreed. But please give me an illustration.

M.: How can it be described? If you dive into water for recovering an article you speak of its recovery only after rising out of the water. You do not say anything while remaining sunk in water.

D.: I do not have fear in sleep whereas I have it now.

M.: Because *dvitīyād vai bhayam bhavati*—fear is always a second one. Of what are you afraid?[27]

Nevertheless, the Advaitin conception of deep sleep is so much at variance with the commonsensical view of it that Ramaṇa often encountered tough going in his effort to bring inquirers around to the standpoint. Two examples must suffice to indicate the kind of difficulties he encountered.

M.: Are you within the body or without?

D.: I am certainly within the body.

M.: Do you know it to be so in your sleep?

D.: I remain in my body in sleep also.

M.: Are you aware of being within the body in sleep?

D.: Sleep is a state of dullness.

M.: The fact is, you are neither within nor without. Sleep is the natural state of being.

D.: Then sleep must be a better state than this.

M.: There is no superior or inferior state. In sleep, in dream and in the wakeful state you are just the same. Sleep is a state of happiness; there is no misery. The sense of want, of pain, etc., arises only in the wakeful state. What is the change that has taken place? You are the same in both, but there is difference in happiness.

Why? Because the mind has risen now. This mind rises after the 'I'-thought. The 'I'-thought arises from consciousness. If one abides in it, one is always happy.

D.: The sleep state is the state when the mind is quiet. I consider it a worse state.

M.: If that were so, why do all desire sleep?

D.: It is the body when tired that goes to sleep.

M.: Does the body sleep?

D.: Yes. It is the condition in which the wear and tear of the body is repaired.

M.: Let it be so. But does the body itself sleep or wake up? You yourself said shortly before that the mind is quiet in sleep. *The three states are of the mind.*[28]

The next inquirer was a really tough customer. He was even reluctant to admit his existence to begin with.

D.: Let us take it that I exist.

M.: How do you know that you exist?

D.: Because I think, I feel, I see, etc.

M.: Do you mean that your existence is inferred from these? Furthermore, there is no feeling, thinking etc., in sleep and yet there is the being.

D.: But no. I cannot say that I was in deep sleep.

M.: Do you deny your existence in sleep?

D.: I may be or may not be in sleep. God knows.

M.: When you wake up from sleep, you remember what you did before falling asleep.

D.: I can say that I was before and after sleep, but I cannot say if I was in sleep.

M.: Do you now say that you were asleep?

D.: Yes.

M.: How do you know unless you remember the state of sleep?

D.: It does not follow that I existed in sleep. Admission of such existence leads nowhere.

M.: Do you mean to say that a man dies every time that sleep overtakes him and that he resuscitates while waking?

D.: Maybe. God alone knows.

M.: Let God come and find the solution for these riddles, then. If one were to die in sleep, one will be afraid of sleep, just as one fears death. On the other hand one courts sleep. Why should sleep be courted unless there is pleasure in it?

D.: There is no positive pleasure in sleep. Sleep is courted only to be rid of physical fatigue.

M.: Well, that is right. "To be free from fatigue". There is one who is free from fatigue.

D.: Yes.

M.: So you are in sleep and you are now too. You were happy in sleep without feeling, thinking etc. The same one continuing now, why are you not happy?

D.: How can it be said that there is happiness?

M.: Everyone says *sukhamahamasvāpsam* (I slept happily or was blissfully asleep).

D.: I do not think they are right. There is no *sukha* (bliss). It is only absence of sorrow.

M.: Your very being is bliss. Therefore everyone says I was blissfully asleep. That means that one remains in the primal uncontaminated state in sleep. As for sorrow, there is no sorrow. Where is it in order that you might speak of its absence in sleep? The present wrong identification of the Self with the body has given rise to all mistakes.

D.: What I want is realisation. I do not feel my inherent happy nature.

M.: Because the Self is now identified with the non-self. The non-self too is not apart from the Self. However, there is the wrong notion that the body is apart and the Self is confounded with the body. This wrong identity must be ended for happiness to manifest.[29]

The conflict between the ordinary view of deep sleep and the Advaitin concept of it was not always easy to resolve, but it seems that Ramaṇa wanted to induce this paradigm shift, so to say, in the inquirer, because he wished to use deep sleep as a paradigm of Advaitic experience, as something we experience in the course of our normal living that could be used as a point of reference to render the doctrines of Advaita reasonably plausible.

This view is confirmed and in fact can be illustrated by considering the number of occasions on which he used deep sleep as a metaphor for the Advaitin experience.

(1) The Advaitin experience is said to be nondual. Ramaṇa explains this implicitly with an extended allusion to deep sleep.

> Deep sleep is only the state of non-duality. Can the difference between the individual and Universal souls persist there? Sleep implies forgetfulness of all differences. This alone constitutes happiness. See how carefully people prepare their beds to gain that happiness. Soft cushions, pillows and all the rest are meant to induce sound sleep, that is to say to end in the state of deep sleep itself. The implication is that all efforts are meant only to end ignorance. They have no use after realisation.[30]

(2) It has been claimed that in *mokṣa* one discovers that there is really neither bondage nor freedom.[31] Ramaṇa again draws a parallel with sleep: "Consider your sleep. Are you then aware of bondage or do you seek means of release?"[32]

(3) The state of liberation is said to be a state of perfection. Again Ramaṇa uses the analogy of sleep to make his point: "Were you not in sleep? Why was there no imperfection?"[33]

(4) The ultimate reality in Advaita is considered formless, so is its experience. Again Ramaṇa points to the experience of deep sleep to illustrate this point.

> Did you not exist in sleep? Were you aware of any form then? Were you with form in your sleep? You existed all the same. The 'I' which was in sleep is also now present. You were not the body according to your sleep-experience. You are the same now—that is without body. Being without the body you were happy too in sleep. You are the same now too. That which is enduring must alone be the real nature. There was no body but only experience of happiness in sleep. That endures now too. The Self is bodiless.[34]

(5) The ultimate reality is said to be beyond time and space and is experienced as such in Advaita. Ramaṇa remarks: "The real 'I' is unlimited, universal, beyond time and space. They are absent in sleep."[35]

(6) The state of liberation, like deep sleep, is said to be free from limitations. But that sleep itself is free from limitations wasn't easy for people to grasp!

> The Heart of the Upanishads is construed as Hridayam, meaning: This (is) the centre. That is, it is where the mind rises and subsides. That is the seat of Realization. When I say that it is the Self the people imagine that it is within the body. When I ask where the Self remains in one's sleep they seem to think that it is within the body, but unaware of the body and its surroundings like a man confined in a dark room. To such people it is necessary to say that the seat of Realization is somewhere within the body. The name of the centre is the heart; but it is confounded with the heart organ.[36]

(7) The Advaitin experience is self-certifying. This may be compared with "the fact that you have no limitations in sleep and no question arises"[37]—or no questions arise!

(8) The state of liberation in Advaita is a sinless state, so is sleep. One may say that the state of normal sleep has come into being due to sin,[38] the sin of individual existence, but in the state itself there is no sin.

> To see wrong in another is one's own wrong projected. The discrimination between right and wrong is the origin of the sin. One's own sin is reflected outside and the individual in ignorance superimposes it on another. The best course is to reach the state in which such discrimination does not arise. *Do you see wrong or right in your sleep*? Be asleep even in the wakeful state, abide as the Self and remain uncontaminated by what goes on around. Your silence will have more effect than your words and deeds. That is the development

> of will-power. Then the world becomes the Kingdom of Heaven, which is within you.[39]

(9) The ultimate reality is to be found within oneself. "Controlling speech and breath," says Ramaṇa, "and diving deep within oneself as a man dives into water to recover therefrom something which has fallen there, one must find out the source whence the ego rises, by means of keen insight."[40] The following parallel is worth pondering here:

> A man sleeps. He says on waking that he slept. The question is asked: 'Why does he not say in his sleep that he is sleeping?' The answer is given that he is sunk in the Self and cannot speak, like a man who has dived in water to bring out something from the bottom. The diver cannot speak under water; when he has actually recovered the articles he comes out and speaks.[41]

(10) The state of Self-Realization is fearless and "deep sleep is not attended with fear."[42]

(11) Self-Realization is said to represent the realization of Be-ing and "deep sleep," according to Ramaṇa, "is nothing but the experience of pure *being*."[43]

(12) Realization is said to be a state of desirelessness. When this point puzzled an inquirer, Ramaṇa again cited the experience of deep sleep.

> D.: Yes, I understand. But I have a small question to ask. The state of Realisation is one of desirelessness. If a human being is desireless he ceases to be human.
>
> M.: You admit your existence in sleep. You did not function then. You were not aware of any gross body. You did not limit yourself to this body. So you could not find anything separate from your Self.
>
> Now in your waking state you continue to be the same Existence with the limitations of the body added. These limitations make you see other objects. Hence arises desire. But the state of desirelessness in sleep made you no less happy than now. You did not feel

> any want. You did not make yourself miserable by not entertaining desires. But now you entertain desires because you are limited to this human frame. Why do you wish to retain these limitations and continue to entertain desires?[44]

In fact the parallels are so close that at one point Ramaṇa says:

> There is only one consciousness subsisting in the states of waking, dream and sleep. In sleep, there is no 'I'; thought arises on waking and then the world appears. Where was this 'I' in sleep? Was it there or was it not? It must have been there also, but not in the way that you feel now. The sleeping 'I' is the real 'I'. That subsists all through. That is consciousness. If that is known, you will see that it is beyond thoughts.[45]

Statements such as these naturally led some to ask:

> D.: Do you mean to say that sleep is Self-Realisation?
>
> M.: It is the Self. Why do you talk of Realisation? Is there a moment when the Self is not realised? If there be such a moment, the other moment might be said to be one of Realisation. There is no moment when the Self is not nor when the Self is not realised. Why pick out sleep for it? Even now you are Self-realised.
>
> D.: But I do not understand.
>
> M.: Because you are identifying the Self with the body. Give up the wrong identity and the Self is revealed.
>
> D.: But this does not answer my question to help me to get rid of Maya, i.e., attachment.
>
> M.: This attachment is not found in sleep. It is perceived and felt now. It is not your real nature.[46]

Although Ramaṇa would not say that deep sleep is identical with the state of Realization, he did say that if the "deep sleep" state could be realized in the waking state, Realization would ensue. So that one now moves from a paradigm to a program!

> M.: Were you aware of limitations in your sleep?
>
> D.: I cannot bring down the state of my sleep in the present state and speak of it.
>
> M.: You need not. These three states alternate before the unchanging Self. *You can remember your state of sleep.* That is your real state. There were no limitations then. After the rise of the 'I'-thought the limitations arose.[47]

Elsewhere Ramaṇa is even more specific.

> M.: The one then in sleep is also now awake. There was happiness in sleep; but misery in wakefulness. There was no 'I'-thought in sleep; but it is now, while awake. The state of happiness and of no 'I'-thought in sleep is without effort. The aim should be to bring about that state even now. That requires effort.

Sleep	Wakefulness	
Effortless		Bring about sleep even in the waking state and that is realisation. The effort is directed to extinguishing the 'I'-thought and not for ushering the true 'I.' For the latter is eternal and requires no effort on your part.[48]
Happiness	No Happiness	
No 'I'-thought.	'I'-thought	

The logic of the program is explained as follows:

> Because your outlook is externally directed you speak of a without. In that state you are advised to look

> within. This within is relative to the without you are seeking. In fact, the Self is neither without nor within.
>
> Speaking of Heaven one thinks of it as above or below, within or without, since one is accustomed to relative knowledge. One seeks only objective knowledge and hence these ideas.
>
> Really speaking there is neither up nor down, neither in nor out. If they were real they must be present in dreamless sleep also. For what is real must be continuous and permanent. Did you feel 'in' or 'out' in sleep? Of course not.
>
> D.: I do not remember.
>
> M.: If there was anything there that could be remembered. But you admit your existence then. The same Self is now speaking. The Self who was undifferentiated in sleep is differentiated in the present state, and sees the diversity. The Real Existence is the only One devoid of objective knowledge. That is absolute consciousness. That is the state of happiness, as admitted by all of us. That state must be brought about even in this waking state. It is called jagrat sushupti. That is mukti.[49]

The analysis of consciousness constitutes that very core of Advaita philosophy. From this point of view the analysis of the consciousness of deep sleep by Ramaṇa is particularly significant because he makes our ordinary assessment of the state of deep sleep stand on its head. From the point of view of everyday experience we would regard the state of deep sleep as characterized by (1) unconsciousness, (2) ignorance, (3) sheer physical repose, and (4) implicit unawareness. Ramaṇa offers his own take on these.

According to Ramaṇa, the state of deep sleep can be said to be characterized by unconsciousness or lack of consciousness only if we take consciousness to mean *relative* consciousness. He explains:

> Do you not think now? Are you not existing now? Did you not exist in your sleep? Even a child says that

> it slept well and happily. It admits its existence in sleep, unconsciously though. So, consciousness is our true nature. We cannot remain unconscious. We however say that we were unconscious in our sleep because we refer to qualified consciousness. The world, the body, etc., are so imbedded in us that this relative consciousness is taken to be the Self. Does any one say in his sleep that he is unconscious? He says so now. This is the state of relative consciousness. Therefore he speaks of relative consciousness and not of abstract consciousness. The consciousness is beyond relative consciousness or unconsciousness.[50]

Next he tackles the question of ignorance in deep sleep and again offers a very different perspective.

> Again, sleep is said to be *ajñāna* (ignorance). That is only in relation to the wrong *jñāna* (knowledge) prevalent in the wakeful state. The waking state is really *ajñāna* (ignorance) and the sleep state is *prajñāna* (full knowledge). *Prajñāna* is Brahman, says the *śruti*. Brahman is eternal. The sleep-experiencer is called *prājña*. He is *prajñānam* in all the three states. Its particular significance in the sleep state is that He is full of knowledge (*prajñānaghana*).[51]

The experience of rest or repose during sleep is interpreted in Advaita as the experience of bliss or happiness. This is on the assumption that one is in touch with one's self during that state—a state of affairs to which the peculiar fact that we cannot say we are asleep, when actually asleep, is said to attest. In fact two peculiarities may be noticed. One was just pointed out, the other is that with regard to sleep we can make the paradoxical statement—when out of it—that "I did not know a thing" and "I slept well." In the ensuing passage Ramaṇa addresses all these paradoxes:

> . . . with regard to similar consciousness in the deep sleep, every person is known to say "I was not aware

> of anything; I slept soundly and happily". Two facts emerge from the statement (unawareness of anything and the happiness of sound sleep). Unless these existed and were experienced in sleep they could not find expression by the same person in the waking state. Inference also leads to the same conclusion. Just as the eye sees the darkness which remains enveloping all objects, so also the Self sees the darkness of nescience which remained covering the phenomenal world.
>
> This darkness was experienced when it (the Self) emerged in dots of supreme bliss, shone a trice and fleeted away in such fine subtlety as the rays of the moon which peer through the waving foliage. The experience was however not through any media (such as the senses or the mind), but bears out the fact that consciousness does exist in deep sleep. The unawareness is owing to the absence of relative knowledge, and the happiness of the absence of (seething) thoughts.
>
> If the experience of bliss in deep sleep is a fact, how is it that no one among all the human beings recollects it? A diver who has found the desired thing under water cannot make his discovery known to the expectant persons on the shore until he emerges from the water. Similarly the sleeper cannot express his experience because he cannot contact the organs of expression until he is awakened by his vasanas in due course.[52]

One final point relating to consciousness in deep sleep remains to be explored. Even in deep sleep there must exist a layer of awareness that is deeper than the consciousness or unconsciousness of sleep, otherwise the sense of awareness of identity the individual possesses through the states of waking, dreaming, and deep sleep will be difficult to explain. Let this be called awareness to distinguish it from consciousness. It is perhaps this that is alluded to in the following dialogue of Ramaṇa:

> Muruganar asked what *prajñāna* is.
>
> M.: *Prajñāna* (Absolute Knowledge) is that from which *vijñāna* (relative knowledge) proceeds.

D.: In the state of *vijñāna* one becomes aware of the *samvit* (cosmic intelligence). But is that *śuddha samvit* aware by itself without the aid of *antaḥkaraṇas* (inner organs)?

M.: It is so, even logically.

D.: Becoming aware of *samvit* in *jāgrat* by *vijñāna*, *prajñāna* is not found self-shining. If so, it must be found in sleep.

M.: The awareness is at present through *antaḥkaraṇas*. *Prajñāna* is always shining even in sleep. If one is continuously aware in *jāgrat* the awareness will continue in sleep also.

Moreover, it is illustrated thus: A king comes into the hall, sits there and then leaves the place.

He did not go into the kitchen. Can one in the kitchen for that reason say, "The king did not come here"? When awareness is found in *jāgrat* it must also be in sleep.[53]

Ramaṇa's analysis of the state of deep sleep from the point of view of Advaita, when placed side by side with our ordinary perspective on it, does raise a host of issues that must now be confronted. It is best to frame them in the form of questions, followed by the answers proposed to the questions.

(1) Does the state of deep sleep represent a form of consciousness or unconsciousness?

It represents a state of consciousness.[54]

(2) Does the state of sleep represent ignorance or 'knowledge' of some kind?

The knowledge possessed in the waking state is to be considered relative or 'wrong' knowledge associated with the individual. "When wrong knowledge is totally absent, as in sleep he remains pure *prajñāna* only."[55] *Prajñāna* means pure knowledge.

The state of deep sleep represents relative ignorance and pure knowledge.[56]

(3) Does one possess what we call awareness in deep sleep or does one lack it at the time? The following conversation between an English lady and Ramaṇa clarifies the point and establishes the presence of awareness in deep sleep.

> D.: The other day you were saying that there is no awareness in deep sleep. But I have on rare occasions become aware of sleep even in that state.
>
> M.: Now, of these three factors, the awareness, sleep and knowledge of it, the first one is changeless. That awareness, which cognised sleep as a state, now sees the world also in the waking state. The negation of the world is the state of sleep. The world may appear or disappear—that is to say, one may be awake or asleep—the awareness is unaffected. It is one continuous whole over which the three states of waking, dream and sleep pass. Be that awareness even now. That is the Self—that is Realisation—there is Peace—there is Happiness.[57]

(4) It is claimed that the empirical being reemerges from deep sleep, so "relative ignorance" must have coexisted with "pure knowledge" in deep sleep. Is this not contradictory?[58]

The following explanation is offered by Ramaṇa:

> Knowledge (*jñāna*) is not incompatible with ignorance (*ajñāna*) because the Self in purity is found to remain along with ignorance-seed (*ajñāna bīja*) in sleep. But the incompatibility arises only in the waking and dream states. *Ajñāna* has two aspects: *āvaraṇa* (veiling) and *vikṣepa* (multiplicity). Of these *āvaraṇa* (veiling) denotes the veil hiding the Truth. That prevails in sleep. Multiplicity (*vikṣepa*) is activity in different times. This gives rise to diversity and prevails in waking and dream states (*jāgrat* and *svapna*). If the veil, i.e., *āvaraṇa* is lifted, the Truth is perceived. It is lifted for a *jñānī* and so his *kāraṇa śarīra* (causal body) ceases to exist. *Vikṣepa* alone continues for him. Even so, it is not the same for a *jñānī* as it is for an *ajñānī*. The *ajñānī* has all kinds of *vāsanās*, i.e., *kartṛtva* (doership) and *bhoktṛtva* (enjoyership), whereas the *jñānī* has ceased to be doer (*kartā*). Thus only one kind of *vāsanā* obtains for him. That too is very weak and does not overpower him, because he is always aware of the *Sat-Cit-Ānanda* na-

ture of the Self. The tenuous *bhoktṛtva vāsanā* is the only remnant of the mind left in the *jñānī* and he therefore appears to be living in the body.[59]

(5) How is it possible to be "blissfully ignorant" in deep sleep from an empirical point of view?

"The unawareness is owing to the absence of relative knowledge, and the happiness to the absence of seething thoughts."[60]

(6) Where does our idea of God fit into this scheme of things?

It doesn't, as is clear from the following.

> D.: Is God only a mental conception?
> M.: Yes. Do you think of God in sleep?
> D.: But sleep is a state of dullness.
> M.: If God be real He must remain always, you remain in sleep and in wakefulness—just the same. If God be as true as your Self, God must be in sleep as well as the Self. This thought of God arises only in the wakeful state. Who thinks now?[61]

(7) If both sleep and *samādhi* involve encounter with absolute consciousness, how do the two experiences differ, if at all.

The physical difference is that in *samādhi* the "head does not bend down because the senses are there though inactive; whereas the head bends down in sleep because the senses are merged in darkness."[62] The psychic difference lies in this that ignorance in the form of veiling persists in sleep but is lifted in *samādhi*.

(8) Then does the *jñānī* dream or sleep?

At one point Ramaṇa considered the question inadmissible.

> Sri Bhagavan went out for a few minutes. On his return the same man asked:
> Self-realised *jñānīs* are seen to take food and do actions like others. Do they similarly experience the states of dream and of sleep?
> M.: Why do you seek to know the state of others, may be *jñānīs*? What do you gain by knowing about others? You must seek to know your own real nature.
> Who do you think you are? Evidently, the body.

> D.: Yes.
>
> M.: Similarly, you take the *jñānī* to be the visible body whereon the actions are superimposed by you. That makes you put these questions. The *jñānī* himself does not ask if he has the dream or sleep state. He has no doubts himself. The doubts are in you. This must convince you of your wrong premises. The *jñānī* is not the body. He is the Self of all.
>
> The sleep, dream, *samādhi*, etc., are all states of the *ajñānīs*. The Self is free from all these. Here is the answer for the former question also.[63]

But elsewhere he admitted that the *jñānī* has dreams, and he sleeps because the "tenuous *bhoktṛtva vāsanā* is the only remnant of the mind left in the *jñānī* and he therefore appears to be living in the body."[64]

(9) Is not the "sleep state really dull, whereas the waking state is full of beautiful and interesting things?"[65]

Ramaṇa pointed out that if "sleep" could be brought down into the waking state, one would discover that "it is not dullness; but it is Bliss."[66]

(10) How is sleep different from death?

Firstly, sleep pertains to the same body, death involves another body. Secondly, the transmigration to another body is involved in death; thus although one seems to be in deep sleep in death, it involves a process akin to dreaming.[67] However, they are both similar in being involuntary. "At times," says Ramaṇa, "we merge into the source unconsciously, as in sleep, death, swoon, etc. What is contemplation? It is merging into the source *consciously*."[68]

(11) What is the difference between sleep and fainting?

Ramaṇa explains that "Sleep is sudden and overpowers the person forcibly. A faint is slower and there is a tinge of resistance kept up. Realisation is possible in faint but impossible in dream."[69]

(12) If the mind does not function in deep sleep, how does one *remember* having slept?

Deep sleep is experienced through "*māyākaraṇa* as opposed to the *antaḥkaraṇa* to which we are accustomed in our other states. The *same* instruments are called *differently* in different states . . ."[70]

(13) If deep sleep shares so many features of pure consciousness, "is one no nearer to Pure Consciousness in deep sleep than in the waking state?"[71]

At one point Ramaṇa does not concede this, rephrasing the question to answer it thus: "The question might as well be: Am I nearer to myself in my sleep than in my waking state?"[72] But he concedes that "*Relatively speaking* . . . the sleep state" may be "nearer to Pure Consciousness than the waking state."[73] But it is problematical to leave the matter at that because deep sleep can be an obstacle to Realization. Ramaṇa clearly states in relation to such obstacles: "Sleep is one of them."[74] Elsewhere he remarks: "Does sleep lead you to *mukti*? It is wrong to suppose that simple inactivity leads one to *mukti*."[75] Moreover, not only the aspiration for liberation "arises only in the waking state,"[76] it can "only take place in the waking state."[77]

This somewhat extended discussion was designed to exhibit the illustrative versatility of deep sleep in its modern exposition by Ramaṇa Maharshi. It might be useful to conclude it with the recognition that even in the case of Ramaṇa Maharshi, the paradoxical aspects of deep sleep, which surfaced in the course of its discussion in classical and medieval Advaita, still persist. This is the paradox that while deep sleep can help explain some aspects of realization, such realization transcends it. This is made pointedly clear in the following piece of dialogue between Ramaṇa Maharshi and an early disciple of his, Sivarrakasam Pillai.

> S.P. Swami, who am I? And how is salvation to be attained?
>
> Bh. By incessant inward enquiry 'Who am I?' you will know yourself and thereby attain salvation.
>
> S.P. Who am I?
>
> Bh. The real I or Self is not the body, nor any of the five senses, nor the *prana* (breath of vital force), nor the mind, *nor even the deep sleep state* where there is no cognisance of these.

S.P. If I am none of these what else am I?

Bh. After rejecting each of these and saying 'this I am not,' that which alone remains is the 'I,' and that is Consciousness.[78]

Conclusions

(1) The role that sleep plays in Advaita Vedānta is, on balance, more illustrative than probative in nature.

The point is that Advaita Vedānta does not investigate the phenomenon of deep sleep itself in any depth, rather it uses the depth and richness of the experience of deep sleep to present its own philosophical propositions more persuasively. This may not come as a surprise, for Advaita after all is philosophical and not a psychological system (although it might well possess its own psychology). One may, however, still wish to make the point that it *could* have shown greater *psychological* interest in it, because it comes so close to being a metaphor of its fundamental philosophical claim about the existence of an objectless consciousness. One may, for instance, for this reason, display greater tolerance for its lack of psychological investigation of dreams. Dreams, because they are characterized by a plural consciousness, do not differ radically from the experience of everyday life in this respect. But deep sleep does. So I think the point holds. It could have been analyzed more thoroughly, although it would be anachronistic to say that it could have been 'psychoanalyzed' more thoroughly.

(2) The classification system of Advaita Vedānta in terms of consciousness may have implications for its understanding of consciousness itself.

The classification of consciousness in Advaita Vedānta is famously threefold—(1) *jāgrat*, (2) *svapna*, and (3) *suṣupti*. Note that the state of dream has been distinguished sharply from that of deep sleep in this trichotomy. The question it raises is this: has sleeping been distinguished *too* sharply from dreaming? This statement may itself be considered as an example of the point it is trying to make, for the English verb 'sleep' in a sense includes *both* the period in which one dreams (while asleep), as well as the period in which one does *not* dream, and thus enjoys deep sleep. Sanskrit does not seem to lack a word for sleep in this sense, for *nidrā* would appear to be just such a word. But by focusing so heavily on deep sleep, Advaita Vedānta seems to overlook the fact that the phenomenon of *sleep as such* could help illustrate its favorite doctrines rather felicitously as well. Consider the following statement for instance: Just as the same sleep can be characterized as both with and without dreams, *Brahman* can be described as both *saguṇa* and *nirguṇa*. Could the fact that we do not regularly encounter such a statement in Advaita Vedānta be attributed to the fact that its three states are demarcated so neatly that they do not fully reflect the ambiguity of real life? Is this a case of theoretical clarity taking precedence over an existential lack of it?

Śaṅkara's discussion of a swoon is also helpful in the context of his discussion of sleep, for he tries to distinguish between the two in the course of his gloss on *Brahmasūtra* III.2.10. He writes:

> There now arises the question of what kind that state is which ordinarily is called a swoon or being stunned. Here the *pūrvapakṣin* maintains that we know only of three states of the soul as long as it abides in a body, viz. the waking state, dreaming, and deep dreamless sleep; to which may be added, as a fourth state, the soul's passing out of the body. A fifth state is known neither from Śruti nor Smṛti; hence what is called fainting must be one of the four states mentioned.—To this we make the following reply. In the first place a man lying in a swoon cannot be said to be awake; for he

does not perceive external objects by means of his senses.—But, it might be objected, may not his case be analogous to that of the arrow-maker? Just as the man working at an arrow, although awake, is so intent on his arrow that he sees nothing else; so the man also who is stunned, e.g. by a blow, may be awake, but as his mind is concentrated on the sensation of pain caused by the blow of the club, he may not at the time perceive anything else.—No, we reply, the case is different, on account of the absence of consciousness. The arrow-maker says, 'For such a length of time I was aware of nothing but the arrow;' the man, on the other hand, who returns to consciousness from a swoon, says, 'For such a length of time I was shut up in blind darkness; I was conscious of nothing.'—A waking man, moreover, however much his mind may be concentrated on one object, keeps his body upright; while the body of a swooning person falls prostrate on the ground. Hence a man in a swoon is not awake.—Nor, in the second place, is he dreaming; because he is altogether unconscious.—Nor, in the third place, is he dead; for he continues to breathe and to be warm. When a man has become senseless and people are in doubt whether he be alive or dead, they touch the region of his heart, in order to ascertain whether warmth continues in his body or not, and put their hands to his nostrils to ascertain whether breathing goes on or not. If, then, they perceive neither warmth nor breath, they conclude that he is dead, and carry his body into the forest in order to burn it; if, on the other hand, they do perceive warmth and breath, they decide that he is not dead, and begin to sprinkle him with cold water so that he may recover consciousness.—That a man who has swooned away is not dead follows, moreover, from the fact of his rising again (to conscious life); for from Yama's realm none ever return.—Let us then say that a man who has swooned lies in deep sleep, as he is unconscious, and, at the same time, not dead!—No, we reply; this also is impossible, on account of the different characteristics of the two states. A man who has become senseless does sometimes not breathe for a long time; his body trembles; his face has a frightful expression; his eyes are staring wide open. The countenance of a sleeping person, on the other hand, is peaceful, he draws his breath at regular intervals; his eyes are closed, his body does not tremble. A sleeping person again may be waked by a gentle stroking with the hand; a person lying in a swoon not even by a blow with a club. Moreover, senselessness and sleep have different causes; the former is produced by a blow on the head with a club or the like, the latter by weariness. Nor, finally, is it the common opinion that stunned or swooning people are asleep.—It thus remains for us to assume that the state of senselessness (in swooning, &c.) is a half-union (or half-coincidence), as it coincides in so far as it is an unconscious state and does not coincide in so far as it has different characteristics.—But how can absence of consciousness in a swoon, &c., be called half-coincidence (with deep sleep)? With regard to deep sleep scripture says, 'He becomes united with the True' (*Ch.* Up. VI, 8, I); 'Then a thief is not a thief' *(Br.* Up. IV, 3, 22); 'Day and night do not pass that bank, nor old age, death, and grief, neither good nor evil deeds' (*Ch.* Up. VIII, 4, I). For the good and evil deeds reach the soul in that way that there arise in it the ideas of being affected by pleasure or pain. Those ideas are absent in deep sleep, but they are likewise absent in the case of a person lying in a swoon; hence we must maintain that, on account of the cessation of the limiting adjuncts, in the case of a senseless person as well as of one asleep, complete union takes place, not only half-union.—To this we make the following reply.—We do not mean to say that in the case of a man who lies in a swoon the soul becomes half united with Brahman; but rather that senselessness belongs with one half to the side of deep sleep, with the other half to the side of the other

> state (i.e. death). In how far it is equal and not equal to sleep has already been shown. It belongs to death in so far as it is the door of death. If there remains (unrequited) work of the soul, speech and mind return (to the senseless person); if no work remains, breath and warmth depart from him. Therefore those who know Brahman declare a swoon and the like to be a half-union.—The objection that no fifth state is commonly acknowledged, is without much weight; for as that state occurs occasionally only it may not be generally known. All the same it is known from ordinary experience as well as from the Āyur-veda (medicine). That it is not considered a separate fifth state is due to its being avowedly compounded of other states.[1]

How the experience of deep sleep is to be accounted for in terms of its relationship to similar states thus remains open to debate in Advaita Vedānta.

(3) The location of deep sleep in the different analyses of the human personality found in Advaita Vedānta can be correlated. Let us begin with a general statement such as the following:

> The great Vedantic Acharyas say that in the state of dreamless sleep we actually experience something. This something is not the mere negation of misery and knowledge, as one may suppose from the statement which a man awakening from deep sleep often makes, "I slept happily, I did not know anything". As a matter of fact, one perceives the positive entities, the bliss of the Atman and ignorance itself, in Sushupti. It may be questioned how, without the help of the mind which does not function in deep sleep, the Atman, which by itself is functionless, can perceive these objects. The Acharyas explain it by saying that in deep sleep ignorance is present and functions in a very subtle form, and this reflects the bliss of the Atman, which as Intelligence Absolute is also the Eternal Witness. The

> memory of this experience remains, and that is why we find a man remarks after deep sleep, "I slept happily, I did not know anything".[2]

One positive remark may be made at the outset. The explanation in *Vedāntasāra* draws on *both* the doctrines of the three bodies (*sthūla, sūkṣma,* and *kāraṇa*) and the five *kośas* (*annamaya, prāṇamaya, manomaya, vijñānamaya,* and *ānandamaya*). It is well-known that these are two optional accounts of the human personality, which can be interrelated as follows:

śarīra	*kośa*
kāraṇa	ānandamaya
sūkṣma	vijñānamaya
	manomaya
	prāṇamaya
sthūla	annamaya[3]

Deep sleep displays two apparently *contrary* features: ignorance and bliss. I think Sadānanda quite skillfully explains "ignorance" through the analysis of the *śarīras,* and "bliss" through the analysis of the *kośas,* consistently with the internal logic of the system, so that the last sentence of the citation stands gracefully elucidated. The problem concerns the manner in which the experience *of* deep sleep is to be explained. A similarly elegant explanation is found in *Pañcadaśī* (XI.60) without using the *śarīra* and *kośa* analysis and offered purely in terms of consciousness itself.

What the Advaitins seem to be trying to do is explain the experiences *in* deep sleep. It also seems that, as the Advaitins are committed to explaining all empirical experience in terms of *vṛttis,* they must posit some in deep sleep as well. But one could use *vṛttis* as an explanation without positing them in deep sleep, if one takes the cue from Vidyāraṇya and adapts it for one's own ends. *Pañcadaśī* (XI.64) suggests that a *manovṛtti* (not *avidyāvṛtti*) may become latent in the state of sleep, and one could presumably recover it upon waking. There seems to be no prima facie reason why it should not be deemed to be in suspension—so that that very *vṛtti* continues, though unmodified, in sleep. And if it is a pleasant one on the eve of sleep, as is usually the case, one wakes up feeling pleasant. The idea of bliss in sleep seems to have been overemphasized. In any case, it might be possible to propose such an explanation of it through the doctrine of *cittavṛttis* itself, at least of this point taken in isolation.

But what about the idea of seed or *bīja*? It is quite obvious that empirical consciousness gets unified in some form in deep sleep, and because it is only one, it may appear as none. As Radhakrishnan explains: "In both deep sleep and transcendental consciousness there is no consciousness of objects but this objective consciousness is present in an unmanifested 'seed' form in deep sleep while it is completely transcended in *turīya* consciousness."[4] The point is explained further as follows:

> According to Advaita Vedānta, Reality is one only while the manifoldness of the experiential world is only an appearance wrought by the power of māyā. Suṣupti consciousness is not of the nature of the pure cit that is of the essence of ultimate Reality or Brahman. It contains in its womb as it were in a latent state the subtle objects of the dream world and the gross objects of the waking world. These sets of objects are projected out of it and such projection will be possible only if the projecting agency or māyā is present in suṣupti. In dreamless sleep the experiences of objects and events of the waking and dream states merge in it. They are not destroyed. They are latent in it, in a unitary condition (*ekībhūtaḥ*), to become manifested in their diverse particularities in the dream or in the waking like as the case may be.[5]

When the explanations become overelaborate, they tend to collapse under their own weight, and when they become too many, each seems to cast doubt on the validity of the other. Just to indicate the variety of explanations offered, two more are added to those already indicated. Mahādeva Sarasvatī, apparently a late medieval Advaitin, writes:

> In deep sleep the merits and demerits, which are the causes of pleasures and pains both in the waking state and in dream, become inoperative, and particular cognitions cease because of the cessation of the *jīva*'s conceit in the gross body and the subtle body, but the *buddhi* exists in a causal state in the form of the cessation of all particular cognitions. In deep sleep the internal organ merges in the nescience.[6]

He also "avers that *buddhi* remains in the state of causal nescience in deep sleep while in trance the internal organ remains in its nature in waking state, although in both there is the cessation of particular cognitions."[7] In this explanation *buddhi* is singled out. The famous Advaitin of the sixteenth century, Madhusūdana Sarasvatī gives the following account of *prājña, taijasa,* and *viśva.*

> The universal consciousness conditioned by nescience invested with the potencies of an internal organ and a gross body and unconditioned by them, and the knower of deep sleep is *prājña*. The same consciousness conditioned by nescience and an internal organ, devoid of conceit in a gross body and knower of the dream is *taijasa*. The same consciousness limited by nescience, an internal organ, and a gross body and the knower of the waking state is *viśva*.[8]

But from one point of view, according to him "Ātman exists in sleep as its witness,"[9] an assertion also found in a perhaps later Advaitin work, the *Laghuvasudevamanana,* in which the claim is extended to all the three states:

> In deep sleep the Jiva disappears owning to the absorption of the antahkarana. Then how can he be a witness to that state? As it is the rule laid down in the scriptures that there is only one witness to all the three states, viz., the Atman, which reflects Itself in the Antahkarana, the Atman should alone be known as witness of the deep sleep state. But it is quite evident

> that the Atman is the witness of the waking and dreaming states also.[10]

Although the explanations are basically loyal to the formal stance of the tradition, there are many nuances which make it obvious that the standard description in standard texts of deep sleep or *suṣupti* as "the state of harmonious awareness wherein all distinctions are held in abeyance; the Self as identified with joy (*ānandamayakośa*); the self as constituted by the causal body (*kāraṇa-śarīra*)"[11] must be taken only as a convenient starting point of further investigations.

(4) Some criticisms of the Advaitin position must now be taken into account.

A textual criticism is offered by V. S. Ghate on the basis of the interpretation of the *Brahmasūtra* by Advaitin scholars in the context of deep sleep by implication. We are here dealing with the idea, that, in deep sleep, consciousness assumes a seed form or atomicity, though in its real nature the Ātman is all pervasive. The Advaitin position is that its atomic nature here is "due to its association with the mind," while others have argued that "the subject of the connection of the *jīva* with *manas* or *buddhi* seems to be foreign to the general trend of the *adhikaraṇa*."[12] This argument can also be transformed into a philosophical one by introducing the following consideration: that the Ātman in Hindu thought is either all-pervasive or indivisibly atomic. Thus this attempt to combine atomicity *with* pervasiveness must raise one's philosophical eyebrow, more so because a common concern undergirds both the concepts of the *ātman*, namely, that in neither case is it destructible, for neither the irreducibly small nor the infinitely large can be subject to destruction. Such a concern is absent in the present context.

Other philosophical criticisms of the Advaitin position have also been made, like the one offered by nondualists like Vādirāja.[13] Briefly, the criticism is that according to Advaitins "in deep dreamless sleep the *antaḥkaraṇa* is dissolved . . . the *jīva*, which is consciousness limited by a particular *antaḥkaraṇa*, would be renewed after each dreamless sleep, and thus the fruits of the *karma* of one *jīva* ought not to be reaped by the new *jīva*."[14] This criticism is easily countered from an Advaitin perspective, as the *antaḥkaraṇa* is not said to dissolve in the process but become latent.

An epistemological criticism can also be offered—that "sleep is memory. Such a view belongs to only two schools of Indian philosophy, the Prābhākaras and the followers of Abhinavagupta,"[15] but could be examined further. Similarly, the ontological paradox that in deep sleep one is said to experience *both* the *ātman* as well as its Ignorance could also be more thoroughly addressed.

It is clear then that in focusing on the physiological state familiar to all human beings, and perhaps even all living beings, such as sleep, as a phenomenon to anchor its doctrines both analytically and illustratively, Advaita Vedānta has hit upon a rich vein that it can doctrinally mine virtually endlessly. It has, however, been relatively more successful in exploiting it for illustrative rather than analytical purposes. One must not however underestimate its illustrative cogency. Its invocation can breathe a new life into a philosophical statement just when it is on the urge of expiring from metaphysical exhaustion. It might be appropriate to close this investigation with precisely such an example, drawn from the writings of Śrī Aurobindo.

> But I do not insist on everybody passing through my experience or following the Truth that is its consequence. I have no objection to anybody accepting Mayavada as his soul's truth or his mind's truth or their way out of the cosmic difficulty. I object to it only if somebody tries to push it down my throat or the world's throat as the sole possible, satisfying and all-comprehensive explanation of things. For it is not that at all. There are many other possible explanations; it is not at all satisfactory, for in the end it explains nothing; and it is—and must be unless it departs from its own logic—all-exclusive, not in the least all-comprehensive. But that does not matter. A theory may be wrong or at least one-sided and imperfect and

yet extremely practical and useful. This has been amply shown by the history of Science. In fact, a theory whether philosophical or scientific, is nothing else than a support for the mind, a practical device to help it to deal with its object, a staff to uphold it and make it walk more confidently and get along on its difficult journey. The very exclusiveness and one-sidedness of the Mayavada make it a strong staff or a forceful stimulus for a spiritual endeavour which means to be one-sided, radical and exclusive. It supports the effort of the Mind to get away from itself and from Life by a short cut into superconscience. Or rather it is the Purusha in Mind that wants to get away from the limitations of Mind and Life into the superconscient Infinite. Theoretically, the way for that is for the mind to deny all its perceptions and all the preoccupation of the vital and see and treat them as illusions. Practically, when the mind draws from itself, it enters easily into a relationless peace in which nothing matters—for in its absoluteness there are no mental or vital values—and from which the mind can rapidly move towards that great short cut to the superconscient, mindless trance, *suṣupti*. In proportion to the thoroughness of that movement all the perceptions it has once accepted become unreal to it—illusion, Maya, it is on its road towards immergence.[16]

Notes

Preface

1. *Yogasūtra* I.6. Also see I.10.

2. See Satischandra Chatterjee and Dhirendramohan Datta, *An Introduction to Indian Philosophy* (Calcutta: University of Calcutta, 1950), p. 301–302.

3. Two other aspects of the discussion of sleep in *yoga* also seem relevant. Attention is drawn to them by Andrew O. Fort in *The Self and Its States: A States of Consciousness Doctrine in Advaita Vedānta* (Delhi: Motilal Banarsidass, 1990) as follows: (1) "Betty Heimann makes some interesting remarks about sleep and *Yoga*, arguing that the goal of *yoga* is exactly what occurs 'naturally' in sleep—the cessation of wishes, concepts, and the 'I'. Such cessation brings wisdom and release, according to speculation in the older Upaniṣads. As is made explicit in *Maitri* VI.25, sleep's 'naturally' blissful unity becomes the model for yogic unity. The difference, of course, is that the yogic reduction of perception and painful desires is done by controlled self-restraint, rather than happening 'unconsciously' as in sleep. Thus, the yogin aspires to a permanent detachment from perceptions and desires which is only temporary in sleep.

"This point-of-view is intriguing and partially convincing, yet I have found few references in *Yoga* texts to the blissful unity of sleep or sleep as a model of release; rather, it is referred to as *tāmasic* dullness. While in theory sleep might seem a promising model, yogic experience appears to have shown that in sleep 'nothing happens' (not No-thing happens)" (p. 63); (2) in *Yogasūtra* I.10 "there was evidently some debate about whether or not sleep is a *vṛtti*, as one never 'knows' one is asleep. Vyāsa argues that sleep is remembered in waking, so some notion must be present. One cannot have a notion of absence as utter nothingness, so the notion must be of the absence of waking and dream. Sleep also may be objectless and 'one-pointed,' but it is this way due to being covered by *tamas* (dullness), thus it is far from (and must be restricted to reach) *samādhi*." (p. 69, note 57).

4. Ibid., p. 8.

5. Ibid., p. 1.

Introduction

1. D. B. Gangoli, *The Magic Jewel of Intuition: The Tri-Basic Method of Cognizing the Self* (Holenarasipur: Adhyatma Prakashan Karyalaya, 1986) p. 43.

2. Ibid.

3. Ibid., p. 44.

4. Ibid., p. 45, emphasis added.

5. Ibid., p. 56.

6. Ibid., p. 58–59.

7. Ibid., pp. 93–94.

8. Ibid., p. 101.

9. Ibid., p. 98.

Chapter One

1. Karl H. Potter, ed., *Encyclopedia of Indian Philosophies: Advaita Vedānta up to Śaṅkara and His Pupils* (Delhi: Motilal Banarsidass, 1981) p. 7. Notice that this proposition implies deep sleep as evidence in support of Brahman as blissful pure consciousness. "Concerning this latter point, consider the fact that waking concentration is so tiring, and deep sleep so refreshing. Might it not be that approaching brahman in sleep enlivens one, while wallowing in waking's superimposed conditioning is exhausting?" (Andrew Fort, op. cit., p. 13, note 30). Andrew Fort also notes that "the first mention of sleep as blissful, not using

senses and knowing nothing that I have found is *Śatapatha Brāhmaṇa* X.5.2.11–15" (ibid., p. 25, note 17).

2. Quoted in Eliot Deutsch and J.A.B. van Buitenen, *A Source Book of Advaita Vedānta* (Honolulu: The University Press of Hawaii. 1971) p. 13.

3. William M. Indich, *Consciousness in Advaita Vedānta* (Delhi: Motilal Banarsidass, 1980) p. 97.

4. Andrew Fort, *The Self and Its States: A States of Consciousness Doctrine in Advaita Vedānta* (Delhi: Motilal Banarsidass, 1990), p. 8. For a criticism of this position from a transpersonal psychological perspective as offered by Charles Tart, see ibid., p. 118–119.

5. P. Sankaranarayanan, *What is Advaita?* (Bombay: Bharatiya Vidya Bhavan, 1970) p. 38.

6. Andrew Fort, op. cit., p. 7–8.

Chapter Two

1. Thomas J. Hopkins, *The Hindu Religious Tradition* (Belmont, California: Dickenson Publishing Company, Inc., 1971) p. 38, 45; Eliot Deutsch, *Advaita Vedānta: A Philosophical Reconstruction* (Honolulu: East-West Center Press, 1969) p. 5 note 4.

2. Thomas J. Hopkins, p. 39.

2A. Ibid., p. 40.

3. S. Radhakrishnan, ed., *The Principal Upaniṣads* (London: George Allen & Unwin, 1953) p. 262.

4. Thomas J. Hopkins, p. 40–41.

5. Ibid., p. 46–47.

6. S. Radhakrishnan, ed., p. 265.

7. Ibid., p. 201.

8. Ibid., p. 495.

9. Ibid.

10. Andrew Fort, p. 21.

11. Ibid., p. 60.

12. S. Radhakrishnan, ed., p. 507–508.

13. Ibid., p. 265.

14. Ibid., p. 285.

15. Andrew Fort, p. 17–18.

16. Ibid., p. 19. In the *Bṛhadāraṇyaka Upaniṣad*, Yājñavalkya also presents a more dynamic picture of the relationship between waking and deep sleep in section IV.3, as Andrew Fort notes (ibid., p. 18–19.): "in which Yājñavalkya instructs Janaka about that which is the light (*jyotir*) of the person. According to Yājñavalkya, ultimately the self (*ātman*) is this light. He then describes the *puruṣa* in dreams, asserting that it goes beyond this (waking) world and the forms of death (such as embodiment).

The *puruṣa* has two spatial locations (*sthāna*), here and in the other world (*paraloka*), with a third 'place' or boundary state in between, i.e., dream state. In this 'intermediate place', he sees both worlds; he takes the measure of this (waking) world, breaks it down and reconstructs it himself. He now also becomes self-luminous (*svayaṁjyotiṣ*).

Yājñavalkya stresses the *puruṣa*'s freedom and creativity in dream state. He becomes an actor (*kartṛ*), creating objects such as a chariot, road, or lotus pool, and feelings such as joy or fear. He roams around, seeing good and evil, and enjoys *saṁprasāda* (blissful, serene rest). The meaning of *saṁprasāda* here mixes characteristics of dreaming and deep sleep. It later comes to mean the condition of the self in deep sleep wherein there is no roaming or seeing at all. Still, the emphasis here on enjoyment and detachment is consistent with later conceptions: the *puruṣa*, blissful, is not attached (*asaṅga*) to anything 'seen' in this state.

The ever-unatttached *puruṣa* goes back and forth from dreaming to waking (*buddhānta*, later called *jāgrat*), as a fish passes between two banks of a stream untouched by either. Then, changing the simile from fish to fowl, Yājñavalkya adds that as a falcon becomes weary from flying and returns to its nest, so does the *puruṣa* go to his end (*anta*, perhaps *saṁprasāda*) where he is without desire or dreams."

17. Ibid., p. 49 note 24.

18. S. Radhakrishnan, ed., p. 662–664.

19. Andrew Fort, p. 25 note 20.

20. S. Radhakrishnan, ed., p. 859.

21. Andrew Fort, p. 23.

22. Andrew Fort, p. 27. This point may be more significant than is apparent at first sight, if the following comment is also taken into account (Andrew Fort, op. cit., p. 46 note 2): "There is some question whether or not Śaṅkara takes the MāU to be an Upaniṣad because he never refers to it as *śruti*. He certainly regards it highly: the MāU and GK together are called *'vedāntārtha-sāra-saṁgraha,'* a summary of the essence of the purport of the Vedānta (in his Bhagavad-Gitā introduction, Śaṅkara calls that text *'Vedārtha-sāra-saṁgraha'*). When beginning this commentary, he writes that the four *prakaraṇas* commence with *'om ity etad akṣaram'*, which is the first line of the MāU. Thus it seems that Śaṅkara takes the MāU and GK as one text, and the *kārikās* are surely not *śruti* (the separate numbering could well be the work of a later editor). If the MāU is not *śruti*, one can better understand why the *catuṣpād* doctrine goes unmentioned outside of this commentary. As is well-known, Śaṅkara tries to use 'classic' Upaniṣads like the BāU and ChU to establish his views. This tendency would lead him to use 'ātman' and neglect 'turīya.' "

23. Ibid., p. 29.

24. T. M. P. Mahadevan, *Guaḍapāda: A Study in Early Advaita* (Madras: University of Madras, 1960) p. 99–100.

25. Ibid., p. 99.

26. Ibid., emphasis added.

27. Ibid.

28. Ibid., emphasis added.

29. S. Radhakrishnan, ed., p. 697.

30. S. Radhakrishnan, ed., p. 456. Radhakrishnan has to annotate that in "dreamless sleep, *buddhi* or understanding remains in a potential condition." Nor is the statement a provisional one in a progressive series to be corrected subsequently, as was the case with *Chāndogya* VIII.11.1.

31. M. Hiriyanna, *The Essentials of Indian Philosophy* (London: George Allen & Unwin, 1948) p. 173.

32. Ibid., p. 209. He also cites Śaṅkara's commentary on *Brahmasūtra* IV.1.3.

33. K. Satchidananda Murty, *Revelation and Reason in Advaita Vedānta* (New York: Columbia University Press, 1959) p. 99.

34. Ibid., p. 342.

35. Swami Gambhirananda, tr., *Brahma-Sūtra-Bhāṣya of Śrī Śaṅkarācārya* (Calcutta: Advaita Ashrama, 1965) p. 821.

36. William M. Indich, *Consciousness in Advaita Vedānta*, p. 37, emphasis added.

37. Swami Swahananda, tr., *Pañcadaśī of Śrī Vidyāraṇya Swāmī* (Madras: Sri Ramakrishna Math, 1967) p. 441.

38. S. Radhakrishnan, tr. *The Brahma Sūtra: The Philosophy of Spiritual Life* (London: George Allen & Unwin, 1960) p. 32.

39. Eliot Deutsch, *Advaita Vedānta: A Philosophical Reconstruction*, p. 61.

40. M. Hiriyanna, *Outlines of Indian Philosophy* (Bombay: Blackie & Sons, 1983) p. 71, emphasis added.

41. S. Radhakrishnan, tr., *The Brahma Sūtra*, p. 125.

42. K. Satchidananda Murty, *Revelation and Reason in Advaita Vedānta* (New York: Columbia University Press, 1959) p. 8.

43. Alladi Mahadeva Sastry, tr., *The Bhagavadgita with the Commentary of Sri Sankaracharya* (Madras: Samata Books, 1985) p. 330–331. Some diacritics added.

44. M. Hiriyanna, *Essentials*, p. 163–164.

45. This is how the term *prasthānatraya* is sometimes rendered into English (T. M. P. Mahadevan, *Outlines of Hinduism* [Bombay: Chetana, 1971] p. 140–141). At other times the three texts are, perhaps more imaginatively, referred to as the three 'points of departure' of Vedānta (Eliot Deutsch and J. A. B. van Buitenen, *A Source Book of Advaita Vedānta* (Honolulu: The University Press of Hawaii. 1971), p. 4).

46. S. Radhakrishnan, tr., p. 405.

47. Ibid.

48. Ibid., p. 411, emphasis added.

49. Ibid., p. 409–410.

50. Ibid., p. 410.

51. W. Douglas P. Hill, *The Bhagavadgita* (second edition) (Oxford University Press, 1966) p. 78, note 3.

52. Monier Monier-Williams, *A Sanskrit-English Dictionary* (Oxford: Clarendon Press, 1964) p. 356.

53. P. K. Gode & C. G. Karve, eds., *Principal Vaman Shivram Apte's The Practical Sanskrit-English Dictionary* (Poona: Prasad Prakashan, 1958) Part II, p. 661.

54. W. Douglas P. Hill, p. 150, note 5.

55. Alladi Mahadeva Sastry, tr., op. cit., pp. 77–79. Some diacritics added.

56. R. C. Zaehner, *The Bhagavad-Gita* (Oxford: Clarendon Press, 1969) p. 156–157.

57. *Talks with Sri Ramana Maharshi* (Tiruvannamalai: Sri Ramanasramam, 1984) p. 52, emphasis added.

58. Ibid., emphasis added.

59. Ibid. p. 560–561.

Chapter Three

1. Eliot Deutsch and J. A. B. van Buitenen, *A Source Book of Advaita Vedānta*, p. 119. On the relationship of Gauḍapāda to the *kārikās*, see Andrew Fort, *The Self and Its States: A States of Consciousness Doctrine in Advaita Vedānta* (Delhi: Motilal Banarsidass, 1990), p. 31.

2. T. M. P. Mahadevan, *Guaḍapāda: A Study in Early Advaita*, passim.

3. Ibid., p. 94.

4. Ibid., p. 94–95.

5. Ibid., p. 101.

6. Ibid.

7. Ibid., p. 101–102.

8. P. Sankaranarayanan, *What is Advaita?* (Bombay: Bharatiya Vidya Bhavan, 1970) p. 38.

9. Andrew Fort, *The Self and Its States: A States of Consciousness Doctrine in Advaita Vedānta* (Delhi: Motilal Banarsidass, 1990), p. 33.

10. Ibid.

11. T. M. P. Mahadevan, *Gauḍapāda*, p. 103. According to Mahadevan, "the idea behind locating Viśva in the right eye, Taijasa in manas and Prājña in the ether of the heart, is to show that all the three are to be found in the state of waking itself and also to teach their fundamental oneness. The one self is observed as three in the one body, the one alone is known as threefold." (ibid., p. 104).

12. Ibid., p. 104.

12A. Ibid.

13. Ibid., p. 105.

14. Andrew Fort, p. 39.

15. Ibid.

16. Ibid., p. 41.

17. Ibid., p. 39.

18. Ibid., p. 42–43. It is worth noting here that (ibid., p. 35 note 13): "A difference between Śaṅkara and Gauḍapāda, and one of the reasons Śaṅkara is more important in Indian thought, is the seriousness with which Śaṅkara takes appearance (*vyavahāra*). In everyday existence, it is useful to differentiate 'cosmic illusion' from empirical illusions (particularly errors like seeing the snake in the rope). From *paramārtha*, appearance is fundamentally false, but from everyday 'common sense', appearance should be assumed to be real until shown to be false. For example, one should not treat an oncoming herd of rampaging elephants as illusion. On the other hand, particular mistakes (like the rope as snake) might well suggest the cosmic illusion to us. The affirmation or negation of *vayavahāra* as a whole (versus specific empirical mistakes) brings forth a true 'value judgment.' "

19. Ibid., p. 39.

20. Ibid.

21. Ibid., p. 48.

22. Ibid., p. 55.

23. Ibid.

24. Ibid., p. 56.

25. Ibid.

26. Ibid., p. 67, note 38.

Chapter Four

1. George Thibaut, tr., *The Vedānta Sūtras of Bādarāyaṇa with the Commentary of Śaṅkara* (New York: Dover Publications, Inc., 1962: first published 1896) Part I, p. 273.

2. The other already alluded to is *Chāndogya Upaniṣad* VIII.3.2.

3. George Thibaut, tr., Part I, p. 180.

4. Ibid., Part II, p. 371, emphasis added.

5. Ibid., Part I, p. 234–235.

6. Another passage that deserves to be cited at some length is his gloss on *Brahmasūtra* III.2.9:

> Here we have to enquire whether the soul when awakening from the union with Brahman is the same which entered into union with Brahman, or another one.—The pūrvapakshin maintains that there is no fixed rule on that point. For just as a drop of water, when poured into a large quantity of water, becomes one with the latter, so that when we again take out a drop it would be hard to manage that it should be the very same drop; thus the sleeping soul, when it has become united with Brahman, is merged in bliss and not able again to rise from it the same. Hence what actually awakes is either the Lord or some other soul.—To this we reply that the same soul which in the state of sleep entered into bliss again arises from it, not any other. We assert this on the ground of work, remembrance, sacred text, and precept; which four reasons we will treat separately. In the first place the person who wakes from sleep must be the same, because it is seen to finish work left unfinished before. Men finish in the morning what they had left incomplete on the day before. Now it is not possible that one man should proceed to complete the work

half done by another man, because this would imply too much. Hence we conclude that it is one and the same man who finishes on the latter day the work begun on the former.—In the second place the person rising from sleep is the same who went to sleep, for the reason that otherwise he could not remember what he had seen, &c., on the day before; for what one man sees another cannot remember. And if another Self rose from sleep, the consciousness of personal identity (ātmānusmaraṇa) expressed in the words, 'I am the same I was before', would not be possible.—In the third place we understand from Vedic texts that the same person rises again, 'He hastens back again as he came, to the place from which he started, to be awake' (*Bri.* Up. IV, 3,16); 'All these creatures go day after day into the Brahma-world and yet do not discover it' (*Ch.* Up. VIII, 3, 2). These and similar passages met with in the chapters treating of sleeping and waking have a proper sense only if the same soul rises again.—In the fourth place we arrive at the same conclusion on the ground of the injunctions of works and knowledge, which, on a different theory, would be meaningless. For if another person did rise, it would follow that a person might obtain final release by sleep merely, and what then, we ask, would be the use of all those works which bear fruit at a later period, and of knowledge?—Moreover on the hypothesis of another person rising from sleep, that other person would either be a soul which had up to that time carried on its phenomenal life in another body; in that case it would follow that the practical existence carried on by means of that body would be cut short. If it be said that the soul which went to sleep may, in its turn, rise in that other body (so that B would rise in A's body), we reply that that would be an altogether useless hypothesis; for what advantage do we derive from assuming that each soul rises from sleep not in the same body in which it had gone to sleep, but that it goes to sleep in one body and rises in another?—Or else the soul rising (in A's body) would be one which had obtained final release, and that would imply that final release can have an end. But it is impossible that a soul which has once freed itself from Nescience should again rise (enter into phenomenal life). Hereby it is also shown that the soul which rises cannot be the Lord, who is everlastingly free from Nescience.—Fur-

> ther, on the hypothesis of another soul rising, it would be difficult to escape the conclusion that souls reap the fruits of deeds not their own, and, on the other hand, are not requited from what they have done.—From all this it follows that the person rising from sleep is the same that went to sleep.—Nor is it difficult to refute the analogical reasoning that the soul, if once united with Brahman, can no more emerge from it than a drop of water can again be taken out from the mass of water into which it had been poured. We admit the impossibility of taking out the same drop of water, because there is no means of distinguishing it from all the other drops. In the case of the soul, however, there are reasons of distinction, viz. the work and the knowledge (of each individual soul). Hence the two cases are not analogous.—Further, we point out that the flamingo, e.g. is able to distinguish and separate milk and water when mixed, things which we men are altogether incapable of distinguishing.—Moreover, what is called the individual soul is not really different from the highest Self, so that it might be distinguished from the latter in the same way as a drop of water from the mass of water; but, as we have explained repeatedly, Brahman itself is on account of its connexion with limiting adjuncts metaphorically called individual soul. Hence the phenomenal existence of one soul lasts as long as it continues to be bound by one set of adjuncts, and the phenomenal existence of another soul again lasts as long as it continues bo be bound by another set of adjuncts. Each set of adjuncts continues through the states of sleep as well as of waking; in the former it is like a seed, in the latter like the fully developed plant. Hence the proper inference is that the same soul awakes from sleep. (Ibid., Part II, pp. 147–149).

Another passage that deserves to be cited in toto is Śaṅkara's gloss on *Brahmasūtra* I.4.18, a part of which is excerpted at the beginning of the chapter. It runs as follows:

> Whether the passage under discussion is concerned with the individual soul or with Brahman, is, in the opinion of the teacher Jaimini, no matter for dispute, since the reference to the individual soul has a different purport, i.e. aims at intimating Brahman. He founds this his opinion on a

question and a reply met with in the text. After Ajātaśatru has taught Bālāki, by waking the sleeping man, that the soul is different from the vital air, he asks the following question, 'Bālāki, where did this person here sleep? Where was he? Whence came he thus back?' This question clearly refers to something different from the individual soul. And so likewise does the reply, 'When sleeping he sees no dream, then he becomes one with that prāṇa alone;' and, 'From that Self all prāṇas proceed, each towards its place, from the prāṇas the gods, from the gods the worlds.'—Now it is the general Vedānta doctrine that at the time of deep sleep the soul becomes one with the highest Brahman and that from the highest Brahman the whole world proceeds, inclusive of prāṇa, and so on. When Scripture therefore represents as the object of knowledge that in which there takes place the deep sleep of the soul, characterised by absence of consciousness and utter tranquillity, i.e. a state devoid of all those specific cognitions which are produced by the limiting adjuncts of the soul, and from which the soul returns when the sleep is broken; we understand that the highest Self is meant.—Moreover, the Vājasaneyasākhā, which likewise contains the colloquy of Bālāki and Ajātaśatru, clearly refers to the individual soul by means of the term, 'the person consisting of cognition' (*vijñānamaya*), and distinguishes from it the highest Self ('Where was then the person consisting of cognition? And from whence did he thus come back?' *Bri.* Up. II, 1, 16); and later on, in the reply to the above question, declares that 'the person consisting of cognition lies in the ether within the heart.' Now we know that the word 'ether' may be used to denote the highest Self, as, for instance, in the passage about the small ether within the lotus of the heart (*Ch.* Up. VIII, I, 1). Further on the *Bri* Up. says, 'All the Selfs came forth from that Self;' by which statement of the coming forth of all the conditioned Selfs it intimates that the highest Self is the one general cause.—The doctrine conveyed by the rousing of the sleeping person, viz. that the individual soul is different from the vital air, furnishes at the same time a further argument against the opinion that the passage under discussion refers to the vital air (ibid., Part I, p. 273–274).

The *jīva* is of course caught up in the process of *saṁsāra*. Śaṅkara employs the example of sleep to offer some of the explanations the process seems to require. The question arises, for instance, as to how might the concept of a beginningless yet recurrent *sāmsāric* process be rendered plausible? Śaṅkara has a crack at it during his gloss on *Brahmasūtra* I.3.30 as follows:

> And in the beginningless samsāra we have to look on the (relative) beginning, and the dissolution connected with a new kalpa in the same light in which we look on the sleeping and waking states, which, although in them according to Scripture (a kind of) dissolution and origination take place, do not give rise to any contradiction, since in the later waking state (subsequent to the state of sleep) the practical existence is carried on just as in the former one. That in the sleeping and the waking states dissolution and origination take place is stated Kaush. Up. III, 3, 'When a man being asleep sees no dream whatever he becomes one with that prāṇa alone. Then speech goes to him with all names, the eye with all forms, the ear with all sounds, the mind with all thoughts. And when he awakes then, as from a burning fire, sparks proceed in all directions, thus from that Self the prāṇas proceed, each towards its place; from the prāṇas the gods, from the gods the worlds.'
>
> Well, the pūrvapakshin resumes, it may be that no contradiction arises in the case of sleep, as during the sleep of one person the practical existence of other persons suffers no interruption, and as the sleeping person himself when waking from sleep may resume the very same form of practical existence which was his previously to his sleep. The case of a mahāpralaya (i.e. a general annihilation of the world) is however a different one, as then the entire current of practical existence is interrupted, and the form of existence of a previous kalpa can be resumed in a subsequent kalpa no more than an individual can resume that form of existence which it enjoyed in a former birth.
>
> This objection, we reply, is not valid. For although a mahāpralaya does cut short the entire current of practical existence, yet, by the favour of the highest Lord, the Lords (īśvara), such as Hiraṇyagarbha and so on, may continue the same form of existence which belonged to them in the

preceding kalpa. Although ordinary animated beings do not, as we see, resume that form of existence which belonged to them in a former birth; still we cannot judge of the Lords as we do of ordinary beings. For as in the series of beings which descends from man to blades of grass a successive diminution of knowledge, power, and so on, is observed—although they all have the common attribute of being animated—so in the ascending series extending from man up to Hiraṇyagarbha, a gradually increasing manifestation of knowledge, power, &c. takes place; a circumstance which Śruti and Smriti mention in many places, and which it is impossible to deny. On that account it may very well be the case that the Lords, such as Hiraṇyagarbha and so on, who in a past kalpa were distinguished by superior knowledge and power of action, and who again appear in the present kalpa, do, if favoured by the highest Lord, continue (in present kalpa) the same kind of existence which they enjoyed in the preceding kalpa; just as a man who rises from sleep continues the same form of existence which he enjoyed previously to his sleep (ibid., Part I, p. 212–213).

7. Ibid., Part I, p. 243. Also see Ānandagiri's comment, ibid.

8. Ibid., Part I, p. 312–313.

9. Ibid., Part II, p. 143.

10. Ibid., Part II, p. 144. Śaṅkara then proceeds to resolve the question of where deep sleep is to be located as follows:

> Among these three again Brahman alone is the lasting place of deep sleep; the nāḍīs and the pericardium are mere roads leading to it. Moreover (to explain further the difference of the manner in which the soul, in deep sleep, enters into the nāḍīs, the pericardium and Brahman respectively), the nāḍīs and the pericardium are (in deep sleep) merely the abode of the limiting adjuncts of the soul; in them the soul's organs abide. For apart from its connexion with the limiting adjuncts it is impossible for the soul in itself to abide anywhere, because being non-different from Brahman it rests in its own glory. And if we say that, in deep sleep it abides in Brahman we do not mean thereby that there is a difference between abode and that which abides, but that there is absolute identity of the two. For the text says, 'With that

which is he becomes united, he is gone to his Self;' which means that the sleeping person has entered into his true nature.—It cannot, moreover, be said that the soul is at any time not united with Brahman—for its true nature can never pass away—; but considering that in the state of waking and that of dreaming it passes, owing to the contact with its limiting adjuncts, into something else, as it were, it may be said that when those adjuncts cease in deep sleep it passes back into its true nature. Hence it would be entirely wrong to assume that , in deep sleep, it sometimes becomes united with Brahman and sometimes not. Moreover, even if we admit that there are different places for the soul in deep sleep, still there does not result, from that difference of place, any difference in the quality of deep sleep which is in all cases characterised by the cessation of special cognition; it is, therefore, more appropriate to say that the soul does (in deep sleep) not cognize on account of its oneness, having become united with Brahman; according to the Śruti, 'How should he know another?' (*Bri.* Up. IV, 5, 15).—If, further, the sleeping soul did rest in the nāḍīs and the purītat, it would be impossible to assign any reason for its not cognizing, because in that case it would continue to have diversity for its object; according to the Śruti, 'When there is, as it were, duality, then one sees the other,' &c.—But in the case of him also who has diversity for his object, great distance and the like may be reasons for absence of cognition!—What you say might indeed apply to our case if the soul were acknowledged to be limited in itself; then its case would be analogous to that of Vishṇumitra, who, when staying in a foreign land, cannot see his home. But, apart from its adjuncts, the soul knows no limitation.—Well, then, great distance, &c., residing in the adjuncts may be the reason of non-cognition!—Yes, but that leads us to the conclusion already arrived at, viz. that the soul does not cognize when, the limiting adjuncts having ceased, it has become one with Brahman.

Nor do we finally maintain that the nāḍīs, the pericardium, and Brahman are to be added to each other as being equally places of deep sleep. For by the knowledge that the nāḍīs and the pericardium are places of sleep, nothing is gained, as scripture teaches neither that some special fruit is connected with that knowledge nor that it is the subordinate member of some work, &c., connected with certain results. We, on the other hand, do want to prove that that Brahman is the lasting abode of the soul in the state of deep sleep; that is a knowledge which has its own uses, viz. the ascertainment of Brahman being the Self of the soul, and the ascertainment of the soul being essentially non-connected with the worlds that appear in the waking and in the dreaming state. Hence the Self alone is the place of deep sleep (ibid., Part II, p. 144–146).

11. Ibid., Part I, p. 164.

12. Ibid., Part I, p. 163.

13. Ibid., Part I, p. 168.

14. M. Hiriyanna, *The Essentials of Indian Philosophy* (London: George Allen & Unwin, 1948), p. 124

15. Karl H. Potter, ed., op. cit., p. 93.

16. William Indich, op. cit., p. 98.

17. Ibid.

18. Ibid., p. 99.

19. Ibid.

20. Satischandra Chatterjee and Dhirendramohan Datta, *An Introduction to Indian Philosophy* (Calcutta: University of Calcutta, 1950), p. 301–302.

21. Eliot Deutsch, *Advaita Vedānta: A Philosophical Reconstruction* (Honolulu: East-West Center Press, 1969) p. 61, note 24.

22. P. Sankaranarayanan, *What is Advaita?* (Bombay: Bharatiya Vidya Bhavan, 1970), p. 37–38: " . . . it may be asked if there is not a break in the consciousness of the individual between the time when he lapsed into sleep and the time he woke up from it? If the intervening state during sleep has been devoid of *bahir prajñā* and *antaḥprajñā*, how is the man entitled to say 'I slept well' as if the one who went to sleep and the one who woke from it were the same person? How can there be identity of personality? In this context, Vedanta psychology uses the word *pratya-bhijñā* or recognition of identity. It is of the form: I who lapsed into sleep and I who woke from sleep, both are identical with the individual who was asleep. 'I am he' (*soham*). Even as when a person feels his personal identity

through his infancy, childhood, boyhood, youth, manhood and old age, so too does a man get awareness of his personal identity about what he was before, during and after sleep. This shows that the state of sleep is not one of mental vacuum; but that consciousness functions in it as indicated by the fact of *pratyabhijñā*. It is a state of unalloyed simple consciousness unaffected by experiences. It is therefore *prajñāna ghana*, consciousness whole and entire, like sugarcandy compacted of sweetness all over." (Diacritics added).

23. Ibid., p. 42.

24. See William M. Indich, p. 37.

25. Ibid., p. 98.

26. P. Sankaranarayanan, *What is Advaita?* (Bombay: Bharatiya Vidya Bhavan, 1970), p. 231–232.

27. Karl H. Potter, ed., p. 269.

28. P. Sankaranarayanan, p. 229–230.

29. Swami Gambhirananda, tr., *Brahma-Sūtra-Bhāṣya of Śrī Śaṅkarācārya* (Calcutta: Advaita Ashrama, 1965) p. 269.

30. Karl H. Potter, ed., p. 269.

31. Ibid.

32. Ibid., p. 99, note 1.

33. Sri Ramaṇānanda Sarasvathi, tr., *Advaita Bodha Deepika* (Tiruvannamalai, South India: Sri Ramanasramam, 1967) p. 18–19.

34. Karl H. Potter, "The Karma Theory and Its Interpretation in Some Indian Philosophical Systems," in Wendy Doniger O'Flaherty, ed., *Karma and Rebirth in Classical Indian Traditions* (Berkeley: University of California Press, 1980) p. 250–251, emphasis added.

35. Ibid., p. 251, emphasis added.

36. S. Radhakrishnan, tr., *The Brahma Sūtra*, p. 31.

37. Ibid.

38. M. Hiriyanna, *Outlines of Indian Philosophy* (Bombay: Blackie & Sons, 1983) p. 348–349.

39. T. M. P. Mahadevan, *Superimposition in Advaita Vedānta* (New Delhi: Sterling Publishers, 1985) p. 49.

40. Ibid.

41. S. Radhakrishnan, ed., *The Principal Upaniṣads*, p. 662.

42. Ibid., p. 495.

43. Ibid.

44. William Indich, *Consciousness in Advaita Vedānta* (Delhi: Motilal Banarsidass, 1980), p. 97.

45. *Talks with Sri Ramana Maharshi*, p. 580.

46. Swami Sri Ramanananda Saraswathi, tr., *Tripura Rahasya or The Mystery Beyond the Trinity* (Tiruvannamalai: Sri Ramanasramam, 1980) p. 122.

47. Swami Gambhirananda, tr., p. 492.

48. T. M. P. Mahadevan, p. 34.

49. Ibid., p. 604–605.

50. Ibid., p. 605.

51. Ibid.

52. As the main orthodox rival to Vedānta, the views of the Bhāṭṭa School of Mīmāṁsā may be worth recording, even in passing. "In regard to sleep (suṣupti), Kumārila holds a somewhat peculiar view. He admits of course that the self endures in it as other Indian thinkers generally do; but in consonance with his view of knowledge, he regards the self as characterized then by the potency to know (jñāna-śakti). In this, he differs from the Nyāya-Vaiśeṣika, which denies jñāna in every form to the self in sleep. He also dissents from the Upaniṣads because he recognizes no happiness then. The later reminiscence of happiness to which the Vedāntin pointedly draws our attention, Kumārila explains negatively—as due to the absence at the time of all consciousness of pain. If the self were really in the enjoyment of the highest bliss then, it would be impossible, he says, to explain the feeling of regret which a person feels afterwards if he comes to know that by going to sleep he has missed some common pleasure" (M. Hiriyanna, *Outlines of Indian Philosophy*, p. 305).

Chapter Five

1. Andrew Fort, *The Self and Its States: A States of Consciousness Doctrine in Advaita Vedānta*, p. 59.

2. Ibid., p. 68, note 44.

3. Ibid., note 52.

4. Ibid., p. 59.

5. Ibid.

6. Ibid., p. 60.

7. Ibid., emphasis added.

8. Ibid.

9. Ibid., p. 39.

10. Ibid., p.68, note 51.

11. Ibid., p. 100.

12. Ibid.

13. Ibid., p. 60–61.

14. Andrew Fort describes such an attempt in Vidyāraṇya's *Jivanmuktiviveka* as follows (ibid., p. 80): "The second reference is from the *Laghu Yogavāsiṣṭha* and correlates types of *brahma*-knowers with seven stages (*bhūmi*) of *yoga*. The first three stages are in waking, and the fourth in dream. In the fourth stage, one knows directly the unity of *ātman* and *brahman* from the "great statements" in the *Vedānta*. Oddly enough, given this is the dream state, one is said here to realize the falseness of name and form and to ascertain the non-dual reality.

Stages five through seven are then called subdivisions of *jivanmukti*, and are attained by practising *nirvikalpa samādhi*. In the fifth stage (*suṣupti*), one turns inward, beyond particularity, and attains *nirvikalpa samādhi* on one's own, while in the sixth, 'full' (*gāḍha*) sleep, one is awakened by companions (*pārśvastha*). Here one is empty (*śūnya, nirvikalpa*) and full (*pūrṇa, saccidānanda*), 'I' and non-'I'. The seventh stage, *turīya*, is the highest *samādhi*. A *yogin*, known now as *brahmavid-variṣṭha* (greatest of *brahman*-knowers) never comes back (*vyuttāna*) from this state."

15. Eliot Deutsch and J. A. B. van Buitenen, *A Source Book of Advaita Vedānta*, p. 276–277.

16. Ibid., p. 277.

17. Ibid.

18. Eliot Deutsch and J. A. B. van Buitenen, p. 252.

19. Ibid.

20. S. S. Hasurkar, *Vācaspati Miśra on Advaita Vedānta* (Darbhanga: Mithila Institute of Post-Graduate Studies, 1958) p. 230–231.

21. Ibid., p. 244.

22. Eliot Deutsch and J. A. B. van Buitenen, p. 312.

23. Bratindra Kumar Sengupta, *A Critique on the Vivaraṇa School: Studies in Some Fundamental Advaitist Theories* (Calcutta: Firma K. L. Mukhopadhyay, 1959) p. 199.

24. Swami Swahananada, tr., *Pañcadaśī of Śrī Vidyāraṇya Swāmī* (Madras: Sri Ramakrishna Math, 1967), p. 440 ff.

25. M. Hiriyanna, *Outlines of Indian Philosophy* (Bombay: Blackie & Sons, 1983) p. 348.

26. Swami Swahananda, tr., p. 442.

27. T. M. P. Mahadevan, *The Pañcadaśī of Bharatītīrtha-Vidyāraṇya: An Interesting Expostion* (Madras: University of Madras, 1969) p. 178.

28. Ibid., p. 181.

29. Ibid.

30. Ibid., emphasis added.

31. Ibid., p. 182.

32. Ibid.

33. Swami Swahananda, tr., p. 449.

34. Ibid., p. 450.

35. Ibid. The more complex explanation runs as follows. It is offered as a comment on XI.64. Both the translation of the verse and the commentary are reproduced. "The modification (Vṛtti) of the intellect in which, just before sleep, bliss is reflected becomes latent in the state of deep sleep along with the reflected bliss, and is known as the bliss-sheath.

So the bliss-sheath is (1) a Vṛtti or modification of that intellect (2) which had become latent, (3) in the deep sleep state and (4) catching the reflection of the bliss of Brahman (or bliss that is Brahman). Or in other words, the bliss-sheath is the sheath of intellect gone inward; and in going inward it is divested of the sense organs and it catches and retains the reflection of the bliss of Brahman, which the sheath of the intellect has not.

The modifications (Vṛttis) of the intellect are all bright, clear and distinct. But this Vṛtti, the material cause of the Ānandamaya, is not bright, it is vague and indistinct. It is because it has gone latent; and also because (as the next Śloka says) it is interpenetrated by the Vṛttis or modifications of bliss. We must however remember that in all cognitions or experience the Vṛtti of the intellect is always 'tipped with Cidābhāsa' but not in internal cognitions or experience. This being an internal experience Vṛtti is automatically illumined by the witness and not by Cidābhāsa. And the sense-organs having been left behind do not play any part in the enjoyment of the bliss. This makes it inexpressible, unique.

Another point is to be noted here. Here the attention of the Cidābhāsa of Jīva is complete. In this state the experiencer is a latent Vṛtti of the intellect, enlivened and illumined not by the Cidābhāsa but by the witness directly, reflecting its bliss on it. With the help of a Vṛtti, not of intellect but of mūlāvidyā, preventing the complete identity of Jīva and Śiva, the individual and the Absolute and keeping the experience vague, and revealing its (mūlāvidyā's) existence simultaneously" (ibid., p. 454–455).

36. Ibid.

37. T. M. P. Mahadevan, *Pañcadaśī*, p. 182.

38. Ibid., p. 183–184.

39. Ibid., p. 183.

40. K. Satchidananda Murty, *Revelation and Reason in Advaita Vedānta* (New York: Columbia University Press, 1959), p. 258.

41. Swami Rajeshwarananda, compiler, *Erase the Ego* (Bombay: Bharatiya Vidya Bhavan, 1974) p. 22–23.

42. K. Satchidananda Murty, , p. 114.

43. M. Hiriyanna, *The Essentials of Indian Philosophy* (London: George Allen & Unwin, 1948) p. 121.

44. Swami Sri Ramananda Saraswathi, tr., *Tripura Rahasya or The Mystery Beyond the Trinity* (Tiruvannamalai: Sri Ramanasramam, 1980), p. 129.

45. Andrew Fort, p. 81–82: "The most interesting reference to the states quotes Gauḍapāda's *kārikās* (I.13–15 and III.34–35), and differentiates the states, particularly sleep, from *samādhi* (meditative enstasis). As Gauḍapāda says, in waking and dream, non-dual reality appears to our minds as differentiated, while in sleep the seed of mental activity remains amidst ignorance of reality. A mind merely dissolved in sleep is unlike a well-controlled and undivided mind which exists in *samādhi*."

46. Ibid., p. 82: "Vidyāraṇya is quite explicit about the inferiority of sleep to *samādhi*. He notes that bondage and suffering reappear daily after sleep. Sleep is not only not a controlled practice (like *samādhi*); it stops controlled practice. The fourth (*turīya*, equivalent to *brahman*) is more like *samādhi*; it is obtained when misapprehension (in waking and dream) or non-apprehension of reality (in sleep) are destroyed."

47. Ibid.

48. G. A. Jacob, *A Manual of Hindu Pantheism: The Vedāntasāra* (Varanasi: Bharat-Bharati, 1972; first published 1881) p. 51.

49. Ibid., p. 51–52.

50. Ibid., p. 52.

51. Ibid., p. 52–53.

52. In the light of this Eliot Deutsch's following remark seems partly prophetic. "Deep-sleep consciousness is the self as unified and integrated; it is not so much an overcoming of the distinctions that make for activity and desire as it is (like *saguṇa* Brahman) a harmonization and being a witness (*sākṣin*) to them" (*Advaita Vedānta: A Philosophical Reconstruction*, p. 61).

53. Swami Nikilananada, *Vedāntasāra or the Essence of Vedānta of Sadānanda Yogīndra* (Calcutta: Advaita Ashrama, 1968) p. 35.

54. Ibid.

55. Ibid., p. 34–35.

56. M. Hiriyanna, *Essentials*, p. 163, emphasis added.

57. M. Hiriyanna, *Outlines of Indian Philosophy*, p. 367.

58. S. Radhakrishnan, ed., *The Principal Upaniṣads* (London: George Allen & Unwin, 1953), p. 697.

59. "When a man with all his wits about him is wide awake, he is regarded as being furthest removed from the state in which he ought to be,—he being then enveloped in the densest investment of Ignorance. When he falls asleep and dreams, he is considered to have shuffled off his outermost coil; and therefore a dream is spoken of as the scene of the dissolution of the totality of the gross. The objects viewed in dreams are regarded as 'subtle'. When a man sleeps so soundly that he has no dream, he is regarded as having got rid not only of his 'gross body, but also of his 'subtle body;' hence profound and dreamless sleep is spoken of as the scene of the dissolution 'both of the gross and of the subtle body'. But although, in profound sleep, a man has got rid of all the developments of ignorance, yet he is still wrapped in Ignorance itself, and this must be got rid of. He must not, like the sleeper who 'slept pleasantly and knew nothing,' 'enjoy blessedness by means of the very subtle modifications of Ignorance illuminated by Intellect', but he must become Intellect simply—identical with Blessedness. To this absolute Unity is given the name of 'the Fourth'. (Dr. Ballantyne, as quoted in G. A. Jacob, p. 60–61).

60. Ibid.

61. Ibid., p. 697–698.

62. Andrew Fort, p. 84.

63. Eliot Deutsch and J. A. B. van Buitenen, p. 302, 312.

64. Swami Madhavananda, tr., *Vedānta-Paribhāṣā of Dharmarāja Adhvarīndra* (Howrah: Ramakrishna Mission Saradapitha, 1963) p. 167–178.

65. Ibid., p. 192.

66. P. Sankaranarayanan, *The Principal Upaniṣads* (London: George Allen & Unwin, 1953) p. 35.

67. Swami Madhavananda, tr., p. 167–168. The reference to the physiological activity of the person in sleep being an illusory impression of the person who is awake seems like a somewhat curious application of *dṛṣṭi-sṛṣṭi-vāda*. Also see David Godman, ed. *The Teachings of Ramana Maharshi* (New York: Arkana, 1985) p. 189–190.

68. Ibid., p. 168–169.

69. *Talks with Sri Ramana Maharshi*, p. 603.

70. Arthur Osborne, ed., *Ramana Maharshi and the Path of Self-Knowledge*, p. 184.

71. Swami Madhavananda, tr., p. 192–193.

72. Ibid., p. 193.

73. Ibid.

74. S. S. Suryanarayana Sastri, ed., *Vedāntaparibhāṣā* (Adyar: The Adyar Library and Research Centre, 1971) p. 146.

75. Jadunath Sinha, *Problems of Post-Śaṅkara Advaita Vedānta* (Calcutta: Sinha Publishing House Pvt. Ltd., 1971) p. 20.

76. Andrew O. Fort, p. 88.

77. Ibid., p. 88: "The YV passage most akin to Gauḍapāda *is Sthiti khaṇḍa* 19.9–27. It emphasizes the similarity of waking and dream (as in GK II.1–15). Waking is linked with conceptions persisting (*sthira-pratyaya*) for several moments, while in dream state, conceptions do not persist, being seen only for *one* moment (*kṣaṇa*, GK II.14). This persistence is said to be the only difference (*bheda*) in the experience of the states. Later, another difference is mentioned: in waking the sense-openings are 'assailed' (*samākrānta*); there is no such assailing in dream (19.33–4, GK II.15). However, waking and dreaming are the same regarding the 'reality' of what is seen and the limitations of cause and effect.

Sleep (described in 19.20ff.) arises when the individual self is firmly and serenely established, with no mind or sense outflow. When all has totally ceased, one awakens from the three states 'into' *turīya*. Such an awakening is unlike the temporary quiescence of deep sleep, after which mental activity begins again and the illusory world reappears. One is reminded of Śaṅkara as well as Gauḍapāda here."

78. Andrew O. Fort, p. 85.

79. Ibid.

80. Ibid., p. 85.

Chapter Six

1. See Kurian T. Kadankavil, *The Philsophy of the Absolute: A Critical Study of Krishnachandra Bhattacarya's Writings* (Bangalore: Dharmaram Publication, 1972).

2. See S. K. Maitra et al, eds., *Krishna Chandra Bhattacharyya Memorial Volume* (Amalner: Indian Institute of Philosophy, 1958.

3. Kurian T. Kadankavil, p. 19.

4. Ibid., p. 20.

5 Ibid., p. 21.

6. Ibid.

7. R. C. Zaehner, *The Bhagavad-Gita* (Oxford: Clarendon Press, 1969) offers the interesting perspective here that *ātman* in the state of deep sleep may be viewed as resting in *Brahman* and comes into its own on recovering its consciousness in *mokṣa* (as depicted in *Chāndogya Upaniṣad* (VIII.12.3). See Kadankavil, *The Philosophy of the Absolute*, p. 23.

8. Ibid., p. 22.

8A. Ibid.

9. Ibid., p. 25.

10. Ibid.

11. Ibid., emphasis added.

12. Ibid.

13. Ibid., p. 26–27.

14. Ibid., p. 27.

15. Ibid., p. 29.

16. Cited in Andrew O. Fort, *The Self and Its States: A States of Consciousness Doctrine in Advaita Vedānta* (Delhi: Motilal Banarsidass, 1990) p. 103.

17. Andrew O. Fort, p. 104.

18. Ibid.

19. Ibid., p. 104–105.

20. Ibid., p. 108.

21. *The Problems of Spiritual Life: Swami Krishnananda's Conversations with Larry and Sarah Krauss* (Shivanandanagar: The Divine Life Society, 1992) p. 119–120.

22. Andrew O. Fort (p. 102) seems to bypass him in this regard.

23. *Talks with Sri Ramana Maharshi*, p. 399.

24. Ibid., p. 66.

25. Ibid., p. 335.

26. Ibid., p. 246. Diacritics supplied.

27. Ibid., p. 281–282. Diacritics supplied. This description is quite in keeping with the doctrines as found in Chapter XI of Vidyāraṇya's *Pañcadaśī*. The last quotation from the *Bṛhadāraṇyaka Upaniṣad* I.4.2 is often cited by Advaitins, see M. Hiriyanna, *The Essentials of Indian Philosophy*, p. 22; etc.

28. *Talks with Sri Ramana Maharshi*, p. 197, emphasis added.

29. Ibid., p. 258–259. Diacritics supplied.

30. Ibid., p. 175.

31. David Godman, ed., *The Teachings of Ramana Maharshi*, p. 34.

32. *Talks with Sri Ramana Maharshi*, p. 217.

33. Ibid., p. 236.

34. Ibid., p. 265.

35. Ibid., p. 271.

36. Ibid., p. 451.

37. Ibid., p. 321.

38. Ibid., p. 323. Ramaṇa says: "Once I was asked about the Christian doctrine of 'original sin'—that every man is born in sin and can be delivered from it only by faith in Jesus Christ. I replied; 'The sin is said to be in man; but there is no manhood in sleep; manhood comes on waking, along with the thought 'I am this body'; this thought is the real original sin; it must be removed by the death of the ego, after which this thought will not arise.' " Swami Rajeshwarananada, compiler, *Erase the Ego* (Bombay: Bharatiya Vidya Bhavan, 1974) p. 32.

39. Ibid., p. 35, emphasis added.

40. A. Devaraja Mudaliar, compiler, *Gems From Bhagavan* (Triuvannamalai: Sri Ramanasramam, 1985) p. 15.

41. *Talks with Ramana Maharshi*, p. 361.

42. Ibid., p. 365.

43. Ibid., p. 580.

44. Ibid., p. 503.

45. Swami Rajeshwarananada, compiler, p. 40–41.

46. *Talks with Sri Ramana Maharshi*, p. 237.

47. Ibid., p. 221, emphasis added.

48. Ibid., p. 185.

49. Ibid., p. 271.

50. Ibid., p. 266.

51. Ibid., p. 275.

52. Ibid., p. 580–581.

53. Ibid., p. 459–460.

54. Ibid., p. 266, 275.

55. Ibid., p. 276.

56. The ignorance or *ajñāna* of sleep represents *ajñāna* of a special kind according to M. Hiriyanna who explains the point as follows: "Leaving out the authority of scripture, which is usually cited in this connection, we shall consider here two arguments, both of which appeal directly to our experience:

(1) The first of them points out that Māyā is implied in the very attempt of man to philosophize or discover the nature of ultimate reality. We seek to know it, because we are ignorant of it; and it is this ignorance of ultimate reality or *ajñāna* of Brahman, as the Advaita expresses it, that is to be understood by Māyā. If we remember that the term 'ignorance', like 'knowledge', does not become fully significant until the object to which it refers and the subject or person whom it characterises are known, we shall see that the above argument not only points to Māyā as a fact of our experience but also makes its notion specific by distinguishing it from other forms of the same like one's ignorance (say) of a rope which is mistaken for a snake.

(2) The second argument is based upon the reminiscent experience of a person who wakes up from deep sleep, viz., that he slept

happily, and did *not know*. The problem of deep or dreamless sleep is a difficult one. Without entering into a discussion of it, we may say that this experience also involves a reference to ignorance ('not knowledge'), but as obscuring the whole of reality. The point to be particularly noted here, however, is not what the ignorance in question conceals from us; it is rather the exact meaning of its description as 'not knowledge'. It may appear at first sight that it means the absence of all knowledge (*jñānābhāva*); but it cannot be understood in that sense for it would then be a mere blank, and such a state could not be recalled—much less as one of happiness. Hence the expression is then to signify a unique type of *ajñāna* which, while it is totally removable by a right apprehension of ultimate reality, is distinct from the negation of knowledge. If the first argument tells us what Māya is, the present one tells us what it is not; and it is necessary to know a thing in both ways, if we are to know it well". (M. Hiriyanna, *Popular Essays in Indian Philosophy* [Mysore: Kavyalaya, 1952] p. 88–89).

57. *Talks with Ramana Maharshi*, p. 471.

58. The point is of great significance for Advaita in general and is sometimes answered as follows: "The individualization of the self is itself the result of nescience and as such cannot be the determinant of the incidence of nescience which is its very presupposition. Nescience must have a locus and abode and from the evidence of our own experience we find that nescience is a felt fact. This shows that pure eternal consciousness cannot be opposed to nescience. On the contrary it constitutes the only evidence of its being. Opposition is both a priori and empirical. The opposition of being and non-being is felt a priori. But other types of opposition are empirical and as such can be known only from experience. We have found that there is no opposition between pure consciousness and nescience. Pure consciousness means consciousness which is not determined by any objective reference. It is bereft of subject-object polarization. Pure consciousness thus means unpolarized consciousness". Now, "Granted that there is no opposition between pure consciousness and nescience. But how to account for the opposition of nescience as error with knowledge?" The question is answered as follows: "This has puzzled many a respectable philosopher and it has been seriously asserted that the Vedantist is guilty of self-contradiction. But this is due to their failure to distinguish between knowledge and pure consciousness. Pure consciousness is an eternal and transcendental entity. As regards nescience,

it is also asserted by the Vedantist to be associated with the absolute consciousness which is pure and transcendental and undetermined by objective reference. There can be no difference in transcendental consciousness. The difference of one consciousness from another is only possible when it is made specific and particularized by objective reference, in other words, when it is possessed of a specific content and is called knowledge. Knowledge is consciousness in its essence, but it is different as a specific determination is from the genus. The opposition of error is with knowledge and not with pure transcendental consciousness which is rather the proof of it. Error is also a cognition with a distinct content and it is cancelled only by a cognition with an opposite content with reference to the same situation. It is the true cognition which cancels the false cognition. The true cognition is here called knowledge, and the false cognition error. The opposition only holds between them". (Nathmal Tatia, *Studies in Jaina Philosophy* [Benaras: Jain Cultural Research Society, 1951] pp. 191, 192.)

59. *Talks with Sri Ramana Maharshi*, p. 497.

60. Ibid., p. 581.

61. Ibid., p. 196–197.

62. Ibid., p. 84, 358.

63. Ibid., p. 399–400.

64. *Talks with Sri Ramana Maharshi*, p. 497.

65. Ibid., p. 561.

66. Ibid., p. 564. "All this is only illusion. Forgetting the illusion you are freed from it. Though seeming dull you will be the Bliss itself. Your intellect will be altogether clear and sharp" (Sri Ramananada Sarasvathi, tr., p. 115).

67. Ibid., p. 201.

68. Ibid., p. 266.

69. Ibid., p. 201.

70. Ibid., p. 281, emphasis added.

71. Ibid., p. 561.

72. Ibid., p. 562.

73. Ibid., p. 563.

74. Ibid., p. 312.

75. Ibid., p. 221.

76. Ibid., p. 503.

77. Paul Brunton and Munagala Venkataramiah, *Conscious Immortality* (Tiruvannamalai: Sri Ramanasramam, 1984) p. 103. This on the face of it at least seems to contradict the statement about fainting.

78. Cited in Arthur Osborne, *Ramana Maharshi and the Path of Self-Knowledge* (York Beach, Maine: Samuel Weiser, Inc., 1995) p. 85–86, emphasis added. This point may be elaborated as follows (ibid., p. 83–84): "A man is identical with the Self, which is pure Being, pure Consciousness, pure Bliss, but the mind creates the illusion of a separate individuality. In deep sleep the mind is stilled and a man is one with the Self, but in an unconscious way. In *samadhi* he is one with the Self in a fully conscious way, not in darkness but in light. If the interference of the mind is stilled, the consciousness of Self can, by the grace of the guru, awaken in the heart, thus preparing for this blissful Identity, for a state that is not torpor or ignorance but radiant Knowledge, pure I-am-ness.

Many recoil from the idea of destruction of the mind or (what comes to the same thing) of the separate individuality and find it terrifying, and yet it happens to us daily in sleep and, far from being afraid to go to sleep, we find it desirable and pleasant, even though in sleep the mind is stilled only in an ignorant way. In rapture or ecstasy, on the other hand, the mind is momentarily absorbed and stilled in a fragmentary experience of the bliss that is its true nature. The very words indicate the transcending of the individuality, since 'rapture' means etymologically being carried away and 'ecstasy' standing outside oneself. The expression 'it is breath-taking' really means 'it is thought-taking', for the source of thought and breath is the same, as Sri Bhagavan explained when speaking of breath-control. The truth is that the individuality is not lost but expanded to Infinity."

Conclusions

1. *Ramana Maharshi and the Path of Self-Knowledge* (York Beach, Maine: Samuel Weiser, Inc., 1995) Part II, p. 150–152.

2. Swami Nikhilananda, op. cit., p. 35.

3. Ibid., p. 33–34.

4. S. Radhakrishnan, ed., *The Principal Upaniṣads* (London: George Allen & Unwin, 1953) p. 701.

5. P. Sankaranarayanan, *What is Advaita?* (Bombay: Bharatiya Vidya Bhavan, 1970) p. 39.

6. Jadunath Sinha, *Problems of Post-Śaṅkara Advaita Vedānta* (Calcutta: Sinha Publishing House Pvt. Ltd., 1971) p. 20.

7. Ibid.

8. Ibid., p. 32.

9. Ibid., p.16.

10. Swami Tejomayananda, *An Introduction to Advaita Vedanta Philosophy: A Free Rendering into English of 'Laghuvasudevamanana'* (Dhivanandanagar, U.P.: The Divine Life Society, 1972) p. 109.

11. Eliot Deutsch and J. A. B. van Buitenen, *A Source Book of Advaita Vedānta* (Honolulu: The University Press of Hawaii, 1971) p. 310–311.

12. V. S. Ghate, *The Vedanta* (Poona: Bhandarkar Oriental Research Institute, 1960) p. 89.

13. L. Stafford Betty, *Vādirāja's Refutation of Śaṅkara's Non-dualism: Clearing the Way for Theism* (Delhi: Motilal Banarsidass, 1978) p. 90–91.

14. Surendranath Dasgupta, *A History of Indian Philosophy* (Delhi: Motilal Banarsidass, 1975; first published, 1922) Vol. IV. P. 236.

15. P. E. Granoff, *Philosophy and Argument in Late Vedānta: Śrī Harṣa's Khaṇḍanakhaṇḍakhādya* (Dordrecht, Holland: D. Reidel Publishing Company, 1978) p. 49.

16. *Sri Aurobindo on Himself and on the Mother* (Pondicherry: Sri Aurobindo Ashram, 1953) p. 11. Entry dated 2-10-1938. The attempt to understand deep sleep in terms of brain waves and its larger implications is worth noting, although no firm conclusions seem possible at this stage. Andrew O. Fort refers in this regard (op. cit., p. 115–116) to the authors of the book entitled *Yoga and Psychotherapy*: "The authors associate the *catuṣpād* doctrine's four states with specific brain wave patterns. They hold that the more metaphysically profound a state is, the slower the brain waves

are: beta in waking, alpha in dream, theta in deep sleep and delta in *turīya*. Thus, the highest mental state is indicated by the slowest brain waves.

The authors write that dream needs vary with the extent of repression in waking; meditation lessens repression (by slowing brain waves?), and thus the need to dream. Deep sleep, on the other hand, remains relatively constant (two-three hours) for all people; even *yogins* need deep sleep. At this point, the authors report (following *Advaita*) that sleep is the fullest consciousness, and contains the least amount of ego-limitation. It refreshes and renews the sleeper, but is too profound to be remembered in waking.

In a later section, the authors write that the MāU and GK give the most sophisticated and profound teaching on meditation and psychology in Indian literature. *Turīya* is the 'widened' consciousness of deep sleep when brought back through the other states. One is aware of the universe and the ego simultaneously in this 'delta sleep' state. Swami Rama's experience of '*yoga nidra*' (observing the ego sleep) is given as evidence for these assertions; it is also said that the mind (consciousness) exists beyond the brain (nervous system), as many transpersonal psychologists hold."

Bibliography

Primary Sources

Bṛhadāraṇyaka Upaniṣad
Chāndogya Upaniṣad
Kauṣītakī Upaniṣad
Māṇḍūkya Upaniṣad
Praśna Upaniṣad
Bhagavadgītā
Brahma-sūtra (Śāṅkarabhāṣya)
Māṇḍūkyakārikā
Yoga-sūtra

Secondary Sources

Śrī Aurobindo on Himself and on the Mother. Pondicherry: Sri Aurobindo Ashram, 1953.

L. Stafford Betty, *Vādirāja's Refutation of Śaṅkara's Non-Dualism: Clearing the Way for Theism*. Delhi: Motilal Banarsidass, 1978.

Paul Brunton and Munagala Venkataramiah, *Conscious Immortality*. Tiruvannamalai: Sri Ramanasramam, 1984.

Satischandra Chatterjee and Dhirendramohan Datta, *An Introduction to Indian Philosophy*. Calcutta: University of Calcutta, 1950.

Surendranath Dasgupta, *A History of Indian Philosophy*. Delhi: Motilal Banarsidass, 1975; first published 1922. Five volumes.

Eliot Deutsch and J. A. B. van Buitenen, *A Source Book of Advaita Vedānta*. Honolulu: The University of Hawaii Press, 1971.

Andrew Fort, *The Self and Its States: A States of Consciousness Doctrine in Advaita Vedānta.* Delhi: Motilal Banarsidass, 1990.

Swami Gambhirananda, tr., *The Brahma-Sūtra-Bhāṣya of Srī Śaṅkarācārya.* Calcutta: Advaita Ashrama, 1965.

D. B. Gangoli, *The Magic Jewel of Intuition (The Tri-Basic Method of Cognizing the Self).* Holenarasipur: Adhyatma Prakashan Karyalaya, 1986.

V. S. Ghate, *The Vedanta.* Poona: Bhandarkar Oriental Research Institute, 1960.

P. K. Gode and C. G. Karve, eds., *Principal Vaman Shivram Aptes's the Practical Sanskrit-English Dictionary.* Poona: Prasad Prakashan, 1953. Three volumes.

David Godman, ed., *The Teachings of Ramana Maharshi.* New York: Arkana, 1985.

P. E. Granoff, *Philosophy and Argument in Late Vedānta: Śrī Harṣa's Khaṇḍanakhanṇḍakhādya.* Dordrecht, Holland: D. Reidel Publishing Company, 1978.

S. S. Hasurkar, *Vācaspati Miśra on Advaita Vedānta.* Darbhanga: Mithila Institute of Post-Graduate Studies, 1958.

W. Douglas P. Hill, *The Bhagavadgita* (second edition). Delhi: Oxford University Press, 1966.

M. Hiriyanna, *The Essentials of Indian Philosophy.* London: George Allen & Unwin, 1948.

———, *Outlines of Indian Philosophy.* Bombay: Blackie & Sons, 1983.

Thomas J. Hopkins, *The Hindu Religious Tradition.* Belmont, California: Dickenson Publishing Company Inc., 1971.

William H. Indich, *Consciousness in Advaita Vedānta.* Delhi: Motilal Banarsidass, 1980.

G. A. Jacob, *A Manual of Hindu Pantheism: The Vedāntasāra.* Varanasi: Bharat-Bharati, 1972; first published 1881.

Kurian T. Kadankavil, *The Philosophy of the Absolute: A Critical Study of Krishnachandra Bhattacarya's Writings.* Bangalore: Dharmaram Publications, 1972.

Swami Madhavananda, *Vedānta-Paribhāṣā of Dharmarāja Adhvarīndra.* Howrah: Ramakrishna Mission Saradapitha, 1963.

T. M. P. Mahadevan, *Gauḍapāda: A Study in Early Advaita*. Madras: University of Madras, 1960.

———, *The Pañcadaśī of Bharatītīrtha-Vidyāraṇya: An Interesting Exposition*. Madras: University of Madras, 1969.

———, *Outlines of Hinduism*. Bombay: Chetana, 1971.

———, *Superimposition in Advaita Vedānta*. New Delhi: Sterling Publishers, 1985.

G. R. Malkani, *Metaphysics of Advaita Vedanta*. Amalner, The Indian Institute of Philosophy, 1961.

Monier Monier-Williams, *A Sanskrit-English Dictionary*. Oxford: Clarendon Press, 1964.

K. Satchidananda Murty, *Revelation and Reason in Advaita Vedānta*. New York: Columbia University Press, 1959.

Swami Nikhilananda, *Vedāntasāra or the Essence of Vedānta of Sadānanda Yogīndra*. Calcutta: Advaita Ashrama, 1968.

Arthur Osborne, *Ramana Maharshi and the Path of Self-Knowledge*. York Beach, Maine: Samuel Weiser, Inc., 1995 (first published 1970).

Karl H. Potter, "The Karma Theory and Its Interpretation in Some Indian Philosophical Systems," in Wendy Doniger O'Flaherty, ed., *Karma and Rebirth in Classical Indian Traditions*. Berkeley: University of California Press, 1980.

———, ed. *Encyclopedia of Indian Philosophies: Advaita Vedānta up to Śaṅkara and his Pupils*. Delhi: Motilal Banarsidass, 1981.

S. Radhkrishnan, ed., *The Principal Upaniṣads*. London: George Allen & Unwin, 1953.

———, tr., *The Brahma Sūtra: The Philosophy of Spiritual Life*. London: George Allen & Unwin, 1960.

Swami Rajeshwarananda, compiler, *Erase the Ego*. Bombay; Bharatya Vidya Bhavan, 1974.

P. Sankaranarayanan, *What is Advaita?* Bombay: Bharatiya Vidya Bhavan, 1970.

Sri Ramaṇānda Sarasvathi, tr., *Advaita Bodha Deepika*. Tirumvannamalai, South India: Sri Ramanasramam, 1967.

S. S. Suryanarayana Sastri, ed., *Vedāntaparibhāṣā*. Adyar: The Adyar Library and Research Centre, 1971.

Alladi Mahadeva Sastry, tr., *The Bhagavadgita with the Commentary of Sri Sankaracharya*. Madras: Samata Books, 1985.

Sanjay Kumar Shukla, "Sākṣī—Its Nature, Role and Status in Advaitic Traditon." *Indian Philosophical Quarterly* 26:4 [October 1999] 575–587).

Jadunath Sinha, *Problems of Post-Śaṅkara Advaita Vedānta*. Calcutta: Sinha Publishing House Private Limited, 1971.

Bratindra Kumar Sengupta, *A Critique on the Vivaraṇa School: Studies in Some Fundamental Advaitist Theories*. Calcutta: Firma K. L. Mukhopadhyay, 1959.

Swami Swahananda, tr., *Pañcadaśī of Śrī Vidyāraṇya Swāmī*. Madras: Sri Ramakrishna Math, 1967.

Talks with Sri Ramana Maharshi. Tiruvannamalai: Sri Ramanasramam, 1984.

Swami Tejomayananda, *An Introduction to Advaita Vedanta Philosophy: A Free Rendering in English of 'Laghuvasudevamanana.'* Shivanandangar, U.P.: The Divine Life Society, 1972.

George Thibaut, tr., *The Vedānta Sūtras of Bādarāyaṇa with the Commentary of Śaṅkara*. New York: Dover Publications Inc., 1962; first published 1896. Two parts.

R. C. Zaehner, *The Bhagavad-Gita*. Oxford: Clarendon Press, 1969.

Term Index

Subject Index